COLLEGE

UnMazed

Your Guide to
Design & Document
Your Homeschool

by

Dr. Michele Evard &
Holly Ramsey

MEET THE AUTHORS

Dr. Michele Evard is an educational consultant who assists homeschooling families during the K-12 years and college application process. While homeschooling her three children and mentoring others, she co-founded Many Rivers Unschoolers and later served as president of the Voyagers, Inc Homeschool Cooperative and Resource Center. Dr. Evard is an active member of multiple organizations including Independent Educational Consultants Association, National Association for College Admission Counseling, SENG (Supporting Emotional Needs of the Gifted) and the Digital Learning Collaborative.

Contact: michele@evardconsulting.com

https://evardconsulting.com/

Dr. Michele Evard
Homeschool & Online School Specialist, Educational Consultant, Author & Speaker

Holly Ramsey is an educational consultant specializing in working with homeschoolers and their parents to create clear, concise, and compelling college applications and counselor documents. She is a professional member of Independent Educational Consultants Association, where she served in a variety of roles and is a recipient of IECA's Making a Difference Award. Ms. Ramsey is also a member of the Texas Association for College Admission Counseling. In addition to homeschooling her own five children, Holly taught writing to hundreds of homeschoolers through Brave Writer™ and mentored new Brave Writer™ instructors.

Contact: ThoughtfulHomeschooling@gmail.com

https://thoughtfulhomeschooling.com/

Holly Ramsey
Homeschool & Writing Specialist, Educational Consultant, Author & Speaker

TABLE OF CONTENTS

TABLE OF CONTENTS

ACKNOWLEDGMENTS

We are honored to represent homeschooling in this addition to the *College UnMazed* series. Authors birth words, and those words are born of both experience and community. We benefited from and contributed to generous collaboration within home-educating communities over the past 25 years.

We work with many homeschooling families who trust us with their authentic selves and unique educational paths. We particularly want to thank Rachel Adamson, Nicole Buckhanan, and Maryann Casey for allowing us to share portions of their homeschool records. We also extend our heartfelt appreciation toward Jill Harper, Sylvia Jackman, Rose Ellen Mocombe, Lisa Rielage, Jaime Smith, Jennifer Quinn, and Farrar Williams for reading early drafts of this book. They improved it by their clarifying questions and thoughtful recommendations.

We are thrilled for this book to be published under the banner of College UnMazed. Dr. Amanda Sterk took our words and created graphics that made our text bloom with color and pizazz.

From Michele: My husband, Rémy, and I discussed homeschooling long before we became parents; it's been wonderful to have a partner who has also been committed to this journey from the beginning. We followed child-led learning principles and learned so much with and from our children, André, Rose, and Jo, who each took increasing responsibility for their educations and brought us along for the ride. My parents, George and Carole, modeled the importance of learning and are always interested in our explorations. I love you all so much and am so grateful to be part of this family!

From Holly: To my kids, Jack, Nathan, Bryson, Caroline, and Mike, thank you for the joy that comes from being your mom and the adventure that came from being your teacher. My husband Jack loves us all well and valued our choice to homeschool. Thanks for agreeing that the road less traveled provided the more humane path. I wish my parents, Bess and John, had lived long enough to see this book; they would have been so proud. Everything I know about education, I learned from them.

INTRODUCTION TO SECTION 1

Following an alternative educational path can feel rewarding and risky at the same time, especially when you're navigating uncharted territory. This book helps homeschooling families design and document a homeschool experience for the high school years that successfully prepares a student for college. We'll help you determine and articulate your homeschooling philosophy, address your concerns about how to homeschool, and assist you in creating a clear record of your child's education.

If you're homeschooling or considering homeschooling, you're in good company. Prior to 2019, homeschooled students represented about 3.3 percent of the school-age population. Since that time, the numbers have increased. *The Washington Post* reported growth during and after the COVID pandemic (see Figure Intro 1.1).

Figure Intro 1.1: Rate of Growth in Homeschooling

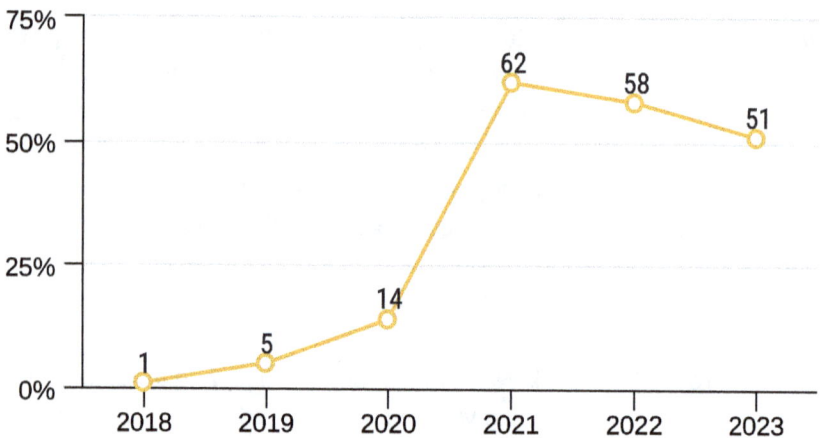

The Washington Post, 2023

The pandemic-related disruption to traditional school fueled this turn to home education, bringing more diversity to homeschooling than ever before. Many people who had never considered homeschooling prior to 2020 found compelling reasons to stick with homeschooling after schools resumed in-person instruction (see Figure Intro 1.2).

Figure Intro 1.2: Reasons for Homeschooling

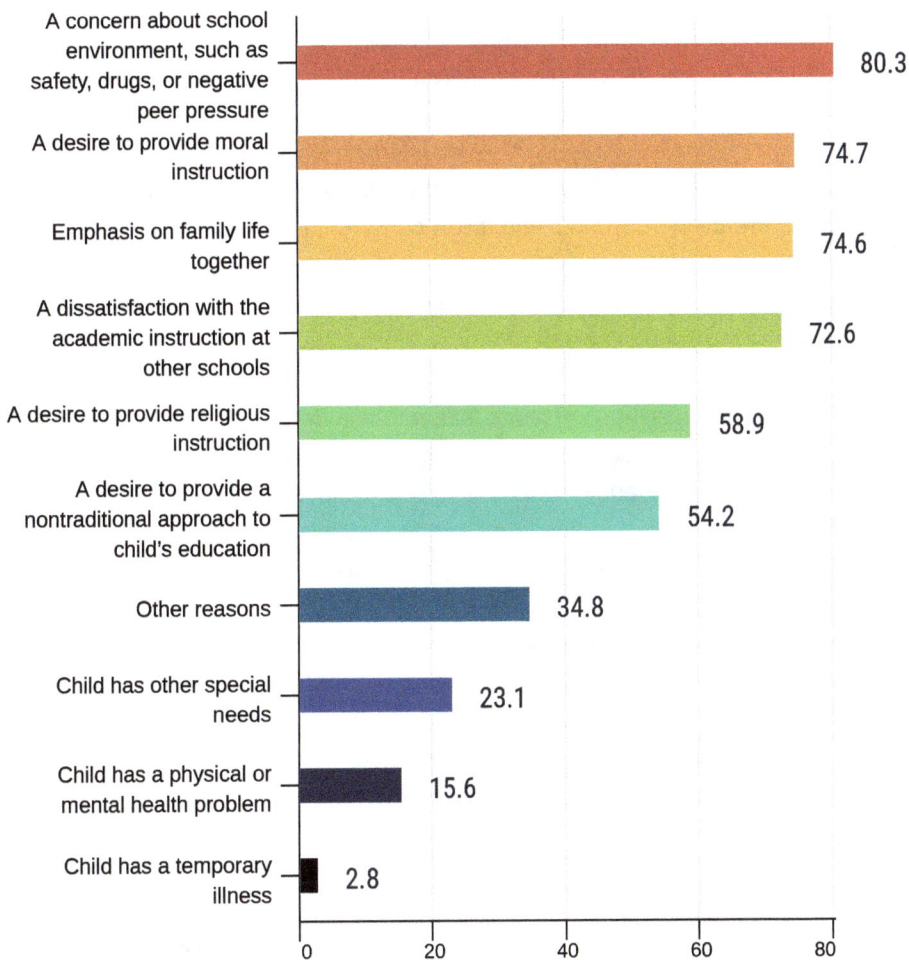

Reason	Value
A concern about school environment, such as safety, drugs, or negative peer pressure	80.3
A desire to provide moral instruction	74.7
Emphasis on family life together	74.6
A dissatisfaction with the academic instruction at other schools	72.6
A desire to provide religious instruction	58.9
A desire to provide a nontraditional approach to child's education	54.2
Other reasons	34.8
Child has other special needs	23.1
Child has a physical or mental health problem	15.6
Child has a temporary illness	2.8

National Center for Education Statistics, 2022

Who Should Use This Book?

There are many legitimate paths teens can choose after graduation from high school. Some teens go directly into internship or apprenticeship programs; others become entrepreneurs, begin work in their field, or obtain certifications. Many families of homeschooled teens want to "keep the door open" in terms of college preparation and documentation. That way, if their child wants to go to college, they can do so and be successful. This book focuses on those homeschoolers interested in applying to college.

Adults who homeschool their children are responsible for providing an appropriate education, keeping records, and making assessments. They also play a large role in their student's college applications. When a homeschooler applies to college, the responsible adult creates and submits the documents that a school would typically provide for the student.

For this reason, this homeschooling companion book to *College UnMazed* is for those who currently homeschool and those considering homeschooling. Although *College UnMazed* speaks directly to students considering college or in the college application process, this book speaks primarily to adults responsible for homeschooling young people.

That said, many homeschooling teens take a role in designing their educational paths, and some even assist in keeping records of what they have done. This can be an advantage when homeschooling high school. One marker of maturity and college readiness is **agency** (see *College UnMazed*, Chapter 1). If you're reading this as a homeschooled student, you are welcome here too!

Are you considering homeschooling?
This book is also for families contemplating a switch to homeschooling from a public or private school. There are many reasons families may choose to homeschool. The one element that all homeschooled students have in common is they have taken an alternative education route for some portion of their education.

In this book, we share examples of some of the many reasons people homeschool and the resources that support their choices. These samples highlight variety rather than indicate endorsement. Some of our example documents are composites from several families and some are from specific individuals used with permission. Readers will notice that not all case studies exactly match our recommendations. Families make their own decisions and tailor their documents to their particular situations. Your reasons for homeschooling and your methods are unique to you, your child, and your family. Quite likely, those reasons, resources, and explanations change just as your homeschool does.

Being outside the traditional system sometimes requires explaining what you do and why you do it, which can feel complicated and be a challenge. However, homeschooling offers the opportunity to present a unique education path to colleges for their consideration. This personalization can help a homeschooled student stand out.

Terms We Use in This Guide
Throughout this guide, we use a number of terms frequently. Some of these terms can carry multiple meanings. We want to clarify the meanings of these terms as used in this book.

Homeschool/homeschooling. When we refer to *homeschool* or *homeschooling*, we mean the educational situation in which a parent or guardian is in charge of both the child's transcript and issuing their diploma.

The legal definition of homeschooling varies from state to state. It is the adult's responsibility to know the laws that govern where they live. In some states, homeschools are considered legal private schools. In other states, the local district has oversight of homeschools. In some states, a department of non-public education regulates homeschools. Several states are highly regulated, and others are nearly devoid of requirements. In this book, we use the word *state* to refer to one of the fifty states, the District of Columbia, or a U.S. territory.

Some schools, including some public schools and many online schools, allow or enable students to learn at home while the school retains educational authority and keeps the records. In these cases, the parent is not responsible for keeping the transcript and the parent does not issue the diploma. For purposes of this book, these students would not be considered homeschoolers.

Many homeschoolers choose to use one or more schools or other outside providers to help meet their students' needs. As long as the family maintains the comprehensive transcript, makes decisions about which providers to use, and issues the high school diploma, these eclectic or flexi-schooling homeschoolers fall under the umbrella of homeschooling. Indeed, research shows that most homeschoolers incorporate one or more providers outside the home.

We use the terms *homeschooling* and *home educating* interchangeably. Although there are completely valid and nuanced philosophical reasons a family might opt to use one term over the other, we see no need to enter that debate here.

Parent/home educator. We use the words *parent* and *home educator* to refer to the adults who are responsible for homeschooling, although in some families this home educator could be a guardian, grandparent, or other trusted adult.

Student/teen/child. We use these terms interchangeably for a young person who is homeschooling for high school, while recognizing that such a learner is not necessarily a teenager.

Credits, courses, and classes. Traditional schools use a credit system to track student progress. At institutional schools, seat time is one typical way to count credit, with one Carnegie credit equaling 120 or more hours and a half-credit equaling 60 or more hours. Some homeschoolers adopt this time-based system for awarding credits.

Many homeschoolers record credit based on mastery of material rather than seat time. This competency-based system awards students credits for learning the material, whether they mastered it in six weeks or two years. In either system, high school Algebra I, for example, receives one credit (as discussed in detail in Chapter 5).

In this book, a *course* and a *class* mean the same thing. A course or class could be one credit or one-half credit, depending on how much material the student learns. We use 1 credit for a typical high school full-year class and .5 credit for a typical high school one semester class. A one-term college class taken through a dual-enrollment (DE) program receives one high school credit.

How to Use This Book
College UnMazed: Your Guide to Design & Document Your Homeschool acts as a workbook with exercises to help you meet your student's goals and match their learning style and preferences. We wrote this homeschool edition based on best practices, current information from colleges and universities, and our own 40+ combined years of experience as homeschool practitioners and as

professional independent educational consultants who coach parents and students through the process.

This book divides neatly into two sections:

- Section 1 (Chapters 1–4) shows you how to homeschool during the high school years. You'll establish goals, plan your homeschool, choose or design courses, keep records, and assign grades.

- Section 2 (Chapters 5–8) teaches you how to distill your teen's homeschool experience into clear, concise, compelling counselor documents that will be submitted with your child's college applications. You will learn to create a transcript, course descriptions, homeschool profile, and counselor recommendation to showcase the strengths of your student's individualized approach.

The Resources section provides sources and additional materials for your use.

You may use this book multiple times. Indeed, we hope you revisit it each year that your child homeschools high school. This book can also serve as a resource for families of younger students who want a preview of their responsibilities as well as for those who are considering homeschooling. Some readers may pick up this book later, at the beginning of the college application process. You will still find it useful to review the first half of the book to understand common high school requirements and guidelines.

Ready to dive in? We have so much we want to share with you. Let's begin!

A Note About Transitions

It's possible that at some point during high school, your teen may opt to attend private or public school on a full-time basis. For some parents, this decision can feel like a judgment of their abilities as a home educator. We offer a reframing: You raised a student who knows and can advocate for their own needs or desires. This quality is necessary for students to thrive in college, and a decision to pursue a different mode of education may have nothing to do with any "lack" on your part.

As a home educator, you probably naturally accommodate any special learning needs of your student. If your child will transition to a public or private school, it's important to work with the school district or other professionals to formalize any necessary accommodations. Such documentation will also be necessary when seeking accommodations for standardized testing.

The teen years are marked by increasing independence. For teens who remain homeschooled, the latter high school years are often marked by increasingly wider boundaries as they sample classes from a variety of sources outside the home. A request to change from homeschooling to institutional school can be another sign of that independence. Be aware that although public high schools must accept your student, they often are not required to accept any of their prior homeschool high school credits. Graduating from an institutional school after homeschooling one or more years of high school may not be feasible. If your teen is interested in this option, it's best to contact your local high school and work directly with the school counselor to understand what is possible.

If you find yourself no longer homeschooling, the tips in Section 2 will still help you document what your student needs to transition to the next phase of high school and beyond.

YOUR HOME
JOURN

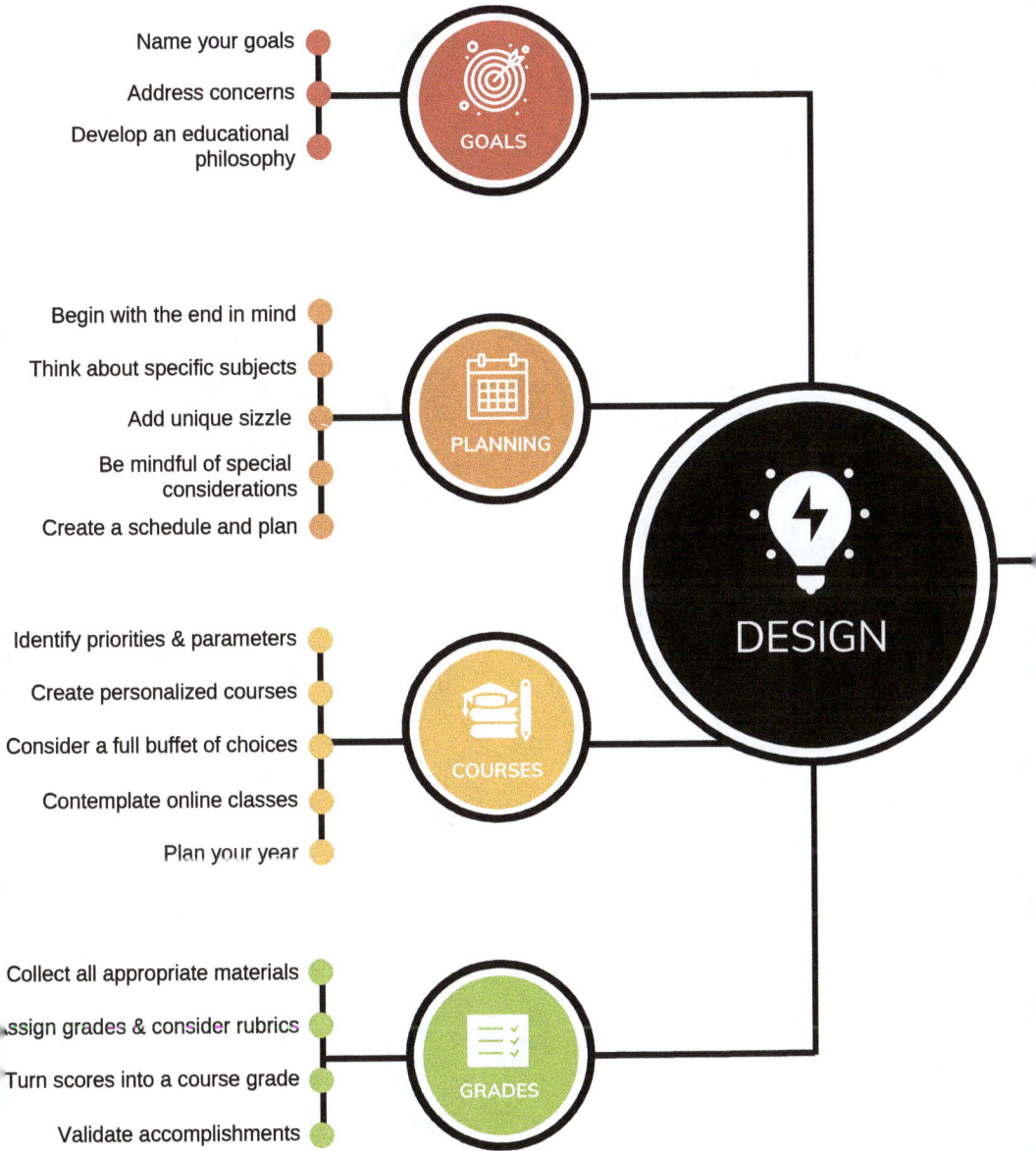

GOALS

- Name your goals
- Address concerns
- Develop an educational philosophy

PLANNING

- Begin with the end in mind
- Think about specific subjects
- Add unique sizzle
- Be mindful of special considerations
- Create a schedule and plan

DESIGN

COURSES

- Identify priorities & parameters
- Create personalized courses
- Consider a full buffet of choices
- Contemplate online classes
- Plan your year

GRADES

- Collect all appropriate materials
- Assign grades & consider rubrics
- Turn scores into a course grade
- Validate accomplishments

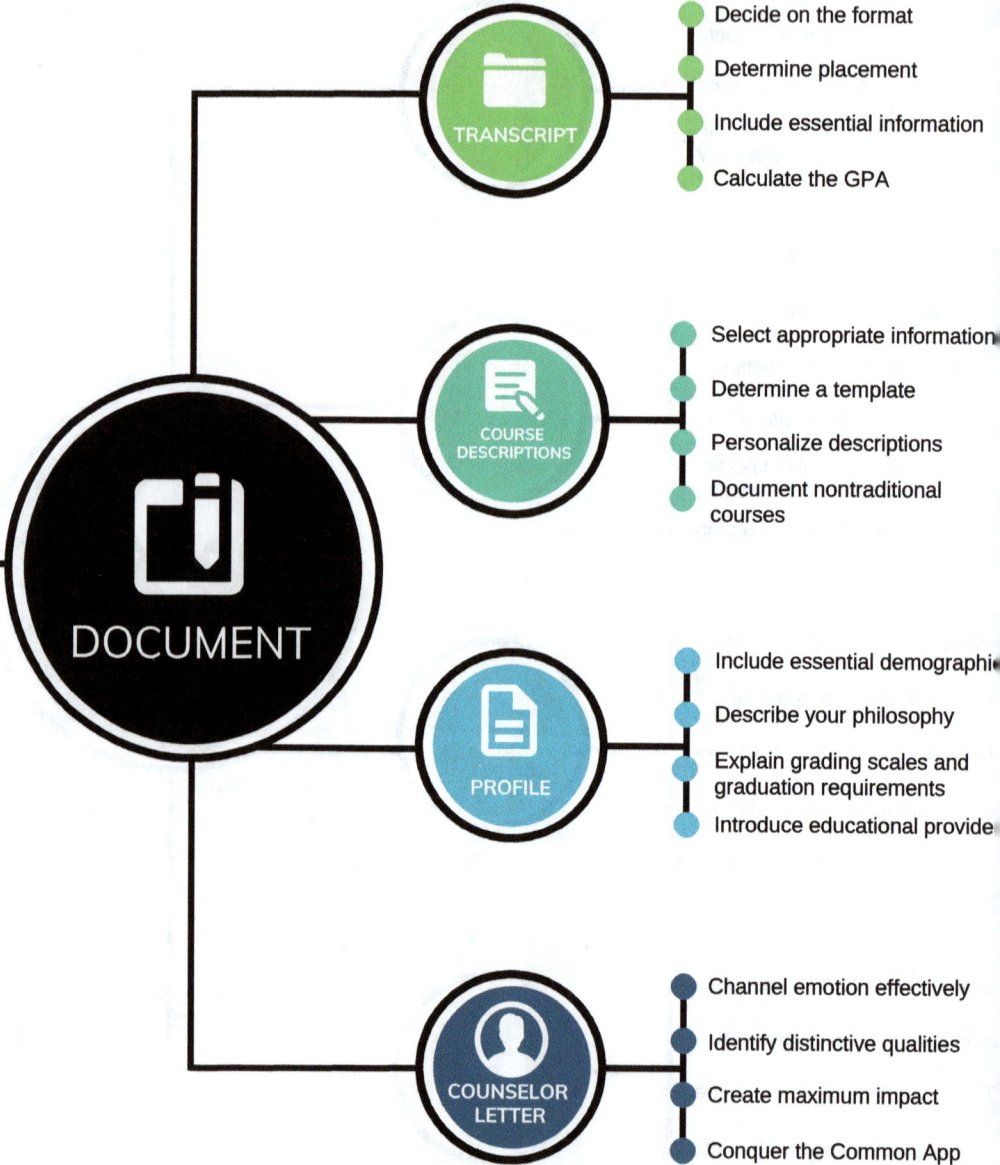

SCHOOL
EY

DOCUMENT

TRANSCRIPT
- Decide on the format
- Determine placement
- Include essential information
- Calculate the GPA

COURSE DESCRIPTIONS
- Select appropriate information
- Determine a template
- Personalize descriptions
- Document nontraditional courses

PROFILE
- Include essential demographic
- Describe your philosophy
- Explain grading scales and graduation requirements
- Introduce educational provide

COUNSELOR LETTER
- Channel emotion effectively
- Identify distinctive qualities
- Create maximum impact
- Conquer the Common App

CHAPTER 1
Goals for Homeschooling
Personalize Your Homeschool

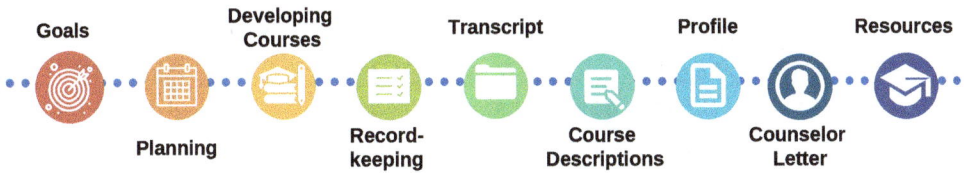

Goals • Developing Courses • Transcript • Profile • Resources

Planning • Record-keeping • Course Descriptions • Counselor Letter

There is no one predefined or widely understood way to homeschool. Home education expert and author Julie Bogart notes, "A lifestyle of learning begins at home—with parents who create a context that is welcoming of children as they are and that offers them happy experiences, accessible tools, and parental involvement." Still, family members, friends, and acquaintances commonly ask many questions.

Why did you start homeschooling?

What about socialization?

Why did your child homeschool for high school?

How did you decide what they should study?

Such queries also need to be addressed when homeschoolers apply for internships or for college. Interviewers and admissions officers are curious too! Thinking through and discussing your reasons for home educating benefits both you and your family. If you don't articulate your thoughts, other people will create their own understanding—or misunderstanding—of what you value and why (see Activity 1.1).

When homeschooling, a parent or guardian takes responsibility for overseeing a young person's education. This chapter encourages introspection about your goals, your child's goals, and how homeschooling will provide opportunities for growth.

Here are some questions to consider:
- Why did you start homeschooling?
- What are your homeschooling-specific goals?
- What concerns do you or members of your family have about homeschooling?
- What can you do to address those concerns?
- How will you answer the common questions?

You don't have to answer all these questions at once or in the order they are listed. Also, note that your answers may change over time.

Activity 1.1: Your Why

Why did you decide to start homeschooling? Write down the reasons that are important to you. Perhaps you are a reluctant homeschooler turning to homeschool to leave or avoid a problematic situation, or maybe you are running toward homeschooling because you see it as a positive educational option. Once you consider your "why," determining your goals becomes easier.

There are three steps in determining your family's path to and through homeschooling:

1. **Name your goals:** You will decide how you want your child to grow through homeschooling across multiple dimensions.
2. **Address concerns:** You will list and address reservations about homeschooling.
3. **Develop an educational philosophy:** You will consider your educational beliefs and core values.

Step 1: Name Your Goals

What are your goals for your child's homeschool experience? What are the steps to make sure you meet those goals? Goals can be long-term, "by graduation" markers or they can exist for a more narrow timeframe of one academic year. Revisiting goals at many points in your homeschooling journey helps keep you accountable and on track.

Some goals fall into the SMART framework (Specific, Measurable, Achievable, Relevant, and Time-Bound) while others are less clearly defined. Both types of goals are appropriate to brainstorm here.

There is no need to limit your answer to academic or future education goals. Although those are important, you can also think about your teen's personal growth, well-being, and maturity. Consider multiple dimensions, including physical, emotional, relational, social, spiritual, intellectual, and vocational ones.

How would you like your child to grow through homeschooling? What strengths and interests do they already have that homeschooling would allow them to develop further? In what areas might they need more assistance?

Figure 1.1: Considerations for Goals

Physical   Emotional   Relational   Social   Spiritual   Intellectual   Vocational

---

The Eight Strengths of College and Career Readiness

When working through Chapter 1 of *College UnMazed*, your child will consider the Eight Strengths of College and Career Readiness and assess their own strengths and areas in which to improve.

If they completed this activity, ask them to discuss it with you. If they haven't, we recommend you consider how you can help them develop in these areas while homeschooling.

As you think about your goals, you may also consider concrete steps you need to take to meet them. You can return to this worksheet over time, as you will learn more about potential steps in the next few chapters as well.

A case study of one family's goals and big picture steps to achieve them is provided in Figure 1.2. This family had three children, one of whom was an athlete, and they tailored some steps to address their individual children's needs while still maintaining their overall family goals. Activity 1.2 will help you determine your own goals.

Figure 1.2: Case Study of One Family's Goals

Goal	Steps to Make Progress
Meet minimum academic standards in all required subjects	• Learn the minimum requirements for our region. • Look for mastery-based standards. • Create a flexible academic schedule that allows our youngest to also pursue athletic excellence while maintaining NCAA eligibility.
Connect to local homeschoolers	• Search for a regional or state-wide homeschool advocacy or support group that has information about homeschooling groups.
Include the 4 Cs of learning: Critical thinking Creative thinking Communicating Collaborating	• Share logic puzzles and brainteasers. Talk about open-ended questions and encourage brainstorming (e.g., What can you do with a brick?). • Look for opportunities to talk with others about their academic interests. • Join or create a homeschool cooperative, book group, etc.

Goal	Steps to Make Progress
Encourage lifelong learning	• Provide individualized learning opportunities. • Encourage my child to pursue their interests beyond the limits of a predetermined curriculum for each subject.
Build relationships with mentors	• Join a homeschool cooperative. • Be on the lookout for adults who have similar interests as my children, and ask if they'll talk with us about their work.
Build practical and career skills	• Look for internships, apprenticeships, and volunteer opportunities.
Familiarize my student with multiple points of view and civil discourse	• Join an inclusive and diverse homeschool cooperative. • Show multiple points of view on one topic, such as through newspapers with different political leanings. • Provide books about life experiences of many people, some who are like our family and many that are not, to build empathy. • As a family, read and discuss *Courageous Discomfort* by McBride & Wiseman.
Encourage intellectual development	• Introduce topics when developmentally appropriate for each child. • Use scaffolding techniques to help them develop skills and move to the next level. • Consider and discuss the ways each child learns different subjects, and provide appropriate means for exploring and learning. • Allow them to work at their own pace when possible, to support accelerated learning or to provide additional time to master a subject.
Foster moral growth	• Treat everyone with dignity. • Talk about faith and belief systems. • Read and discuss appropriate texts. • Join a community that shares our values and commitment to service.

Activity 1.2: Your Goals for Homeschooling

In reviewing the example provided in Figure 1.2, consider what your goals are and the steps needed to make progress. Your goals and your student's goals may change over time. Revisit this worksheet annually during your student's high school years and revise as appropriate.

Goal	Steps to Make Progress

Step 2: Address Concerns

Stereotypes or misconceptions about homeschooling can contribute to worries. In this section, you will face your concerns and articulate how you can overcome them.

One of the top questions asked of homeschoolers is, "What about socialization?" The question invites worry that our children won't know how to interact with people, behave properly in group situations, have friends, or participate in common activities or traditions.

However, socialization does not take place solely in a typical school setting; alternative environments can also provide opportunities to develop the appropriate skills. Young people do not need to attend an institutional school to learn to work in a group or how to communicate well with a variety of other people. Co-ops, field trips, informal classes, multi-age park and museum programs, athletics and other team activities, community groups, and many other activities develop these skills. Parents, other adults, and even older students can model and role play how to enter new social situations.

It can be helpful to think through the sorts of social connections and experiences your child needs and how their needs can be met while homeschooling. Which opportunities will encourage your student to make robust friendships? Where will they meet new people and how will they be able to maintain ongoing relationships with acquaintances and friends? What settings encourage interaction with people of different ages, backgrounds, beliefs, or interests? Will online forums play a role in meeting with people who share their interests?

There is no need to homeschool in isolation. A variety of opportunities will help your child interact appropriately in any setting, treat others with respect, and advocate for themselves. See Figure 1.3 for some ideas. Activity 1.3 will help you identify local opportunities.

Figure 1.3: Ten Example Sources of Social Opportunities

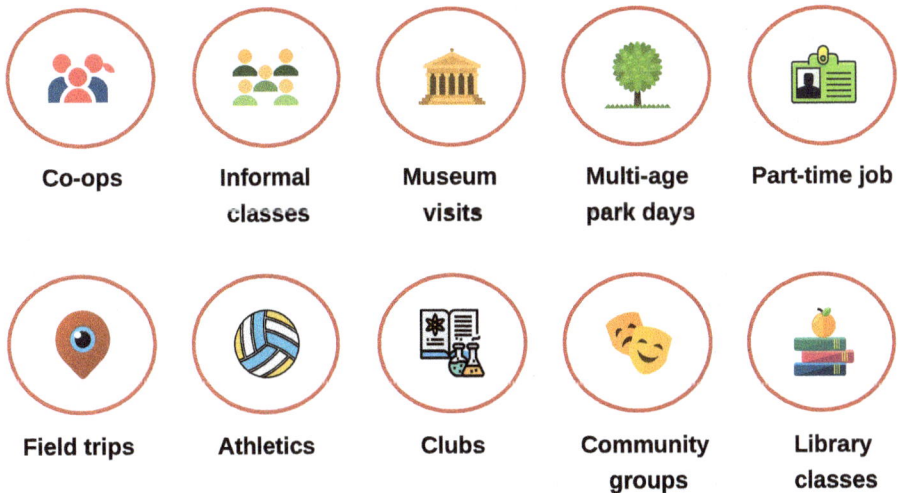

| Co-ops | Informal classes | Museum visits | Multi-age park days | Part-time job |
| Field trips | Athletics | Clubs | Community groups | Library classes |

Activity 1.3: Ways to Connect Socially

To find out more about the various social opportunities available in your area, conduct a little research. Great places to start include any local homeschool co-ops, town recreation centers, social media groups, and other homeschooling families. You can also consider other groups who come together around shared interests or beliefs, whether local or online. Record your ideas in the following chart:

People	Ways to connect
Age peers	
Intellectual peers	
Younger children	
Older people	
Groups	
Mentors	
People with shared interests	
People with different backgrounds	

No educational path, whether institutional school or homeschool, is entirely free from reasons to worry. We address many common concerns about homeschooling in this book, from deciding on graduation requirements to creating a transcript. Other concerns may be personal. For example, one family may have challenges finding transportation to museums, homeschool cooperatives, or community college classes, while another feels distress about the family budget. Some families want to be sure their children participate in some of the rituals associated with school, while others are concerned that their child won't find opportunities to pursue a specific interest. It helps to list your concerns along with some ways that you can address them.

Activity 1.4: Other Concerns

Write down concerns that you want to consider in homeschooling your high school student. We provided an example of one concern we hear often.

Concern	Ways to Address
Example: I want my child to attend prom. Attending prom was important for me, and I want my teen to be able to have this experience.	<ul><li>Find or create a local homeschool prom.</li><li>Look for homeschool conferences that have a prom.</li><li>Provide opportunities to connect to friends who attend traditional schools; be open to my student going to prom in a group or with one of them.</li></ul>

Step 3: Develop an Educational Philosophy

Homeschooling gives families freedom to create an educational philosophy specific to each individual learner. You can adopt a pedagogical approach that works for your family or design your own approach. Either way, think about how your teen likes to learn, not simply how you like to teach. Educational philosophies consider the importance placed on subject matter compared to that placed on individual development, the role of teachers or mentors, and how much independence the learners have. Following are three common philosophical frameworks:

Teacher-directed education is the most common model in traditional schools. A teacher or administration determines the material, method of instruction, and learning objectives. Teachers present information, provide textbooks or other learning resources, give assignments, and assess student work based on predetermined criteria. Students are graded on how well they perform compared to expectations. Classical education generally follows this model.

In **child-centered teaching and learning**, the learner's interests, abilities, and developmental level shape the learning process, including what is to be learned and how progress is demonstrated. Instead of adhering to a fixed curriculum, teachers tailor their classes and assignments to their students. Montessori and Waldorf schools use this method.

In **self-directed learning**, an individual takes primary responsibility for their learning experiences, including planning, learning, and determining how to evaluate their own progress. A few schools use or were inspired by this approach, including The Forest School and Sudbury Valley School. Homeschoolers who use this framework often refer to it as unschooling.

Philosophies of learning that homeschoolers might investigate further are shared in Figure 1.4.

Figure 1.4: Educational Philosophies

- Child-Led Learning
- Classical Education
- Constructivism/Constructionism
- Experiential Learning
- Montessori Method
- Progressive Education
- Project-Based Learning
- Reggio Emilia Approach
- Self-Directed Learning
- Unschooling
- Waldorf Education

Although some homeschoolers ascribe to a single philosophy, others take an eclectic approach incorporating aspects of different philosophies for different subjects. Even the most radically different philosophies can be combined in meaningful ways. A teenager who is an unschooler or self-directed learner may choose to take a college course through dual enrollment. A family who primarily uses teacher-directed learning may honor their teen's desire to self-select a hands-on apprenticeship in a trade.

Many adults have an intuitive sense about what works and what doesn't work for their student. It is helpful to make this issue of effectiveness explicit as you are planning your homeschooling and in the college application process. Here are some questions to get you started:

- In what areas does your student learn by doing?
- When do they prefer learning from reading, watching documentaries, or listening to lectures?
- What topics inspire them to create their own projects, and when might they prefer to fill in a worksheet?
- Are there subjects that require repetition or are there times when doing something a few times is enough?

Much has been made of "learning styles," though recent research suggests that most learners benefit from a multisensory approach.

Your homeschool style may change as your child matures. Your openness to multiple approaches and willingness to change over time is, in and of itself, a homeschooling philosophy.

Activity 1.5: Your Homeschool Philosophy

Consider the following example and then write down your initial thoughts about your homeschooling philosophy. *"Our homeschool provides individualized learning opportunities in diverse environments and encourages our children to go beyond mastery of knowledge and skill to proficiency and deep understanding. As lifelong learners, we share our love of learning with our children while helping them develop critical thinking skills and the ability to direct their own studies."*

Summary

Regardless of the reasons you decided to homeschool, your family needs to address the goals you have, the concerns that might arise, and your overall educational philosophy. You and your student may have differing opinions about how much to share about your homeschooling experience and with whom. Discussing the questions in advance and preparing a short sharable example or two about what your teen is doing or learning can benefit everyone.

CHAPTER 2
Planning Your Requirements
Develop Your Four-Year Program

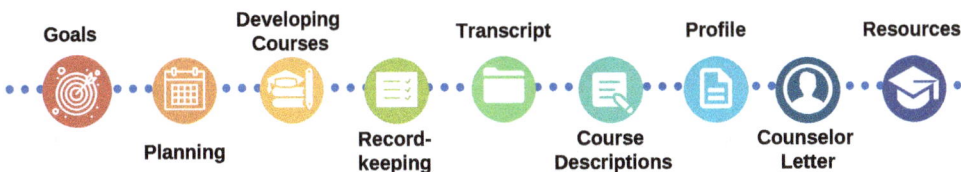

Goals · Developing Courses · Transcript · Profile · Resources · Planning · Record-keeping · Course Descriptions · Counselor Letter

This chapter prepares you to begin homeschooling high school. If your teen already completed any high school classes, first fill out the charts with what they have already done and then use the framework here to determine what additional studies would meet or exceed your graduation requirements.

Homeschooling provides flexibility in what to study and when. Although these choices can feel overwhelming at times, they also let students delve into areas of particular interest and explore broadly. Through their decisions, homeschoolers develop and demonstrate "You Factors" (see *College UnMazed*, Chapter 1).

Some courses are easily defined and described, such as a dual enrollment class or a high school geometry class using a common textbook. Other studies are more challenging to describe in a school format since a homeschooled student learns in many ways. Sometimes you will split interdisciplinary learning experiences into separate "classes" to facilitate explanation; at other times you may bundle a series of experiences together to form one course (see Chapter 6 for additional detail).

You will proceed through five steps when planning your course requirements:

1. **Begin with the end in mind:** You will research your state's legal requirements and typical graduation plans.

2. **Think about specific subjects:** You will explore options for core subject areas and electives.
3. **Add unique sizzle to home education:** You will incorporate your student's particular interests into your plans.
4. **Be mindful of special considerations:** You will factor in any additional requirements for particular situations.
5. **Create a schedule and plan:** You will develop the flow that works for you daily, weekly, and annually.

Step 1: Begin with the End in Mind

How do you figure out what a student should study and when they should learn it? Planning all of high school may seem daunting to the parent of an eighth-grade student. Having a comprehensive strategy helps you know when new opportunities would be an awesome addition to your child's education or if adding them would prohibit your child from achieving a particular goal. Working without an overall plan may result in unintended omissions, missed opportunities, or overemphasis on one subject area to the detriment of others.

First, review any legal requirements in your state. There may be laws, case law, or regulations about homeschooling with steps you must take for your student legally to be considered a homeschooled student. For example, New York requires home educators to file an "individualized home instruction plan" with their local school superintendent. The state of Washington requires schools and homeschoolers to provide "instruction in the basic skills of occupational education." These legal requirements may seem complicated or confusing. A statewide homeschool advocacy or support group may provide clarity. If all students must meet a requirement, check local high schools to see how their students fulfill the mandate.

Visit your state's official education website to determine what is required. Homeschooling groups and school districts may provide additional interpretations of the regulations that can be helpful for reference, but be aware that these secondary sources are not always accurate. Figure 2.1 summarizes the level of homeschool notification required by each state. Activity 2.1 will guide you in your research.

Figure 2.1: Homeschool Notification Requirements by State

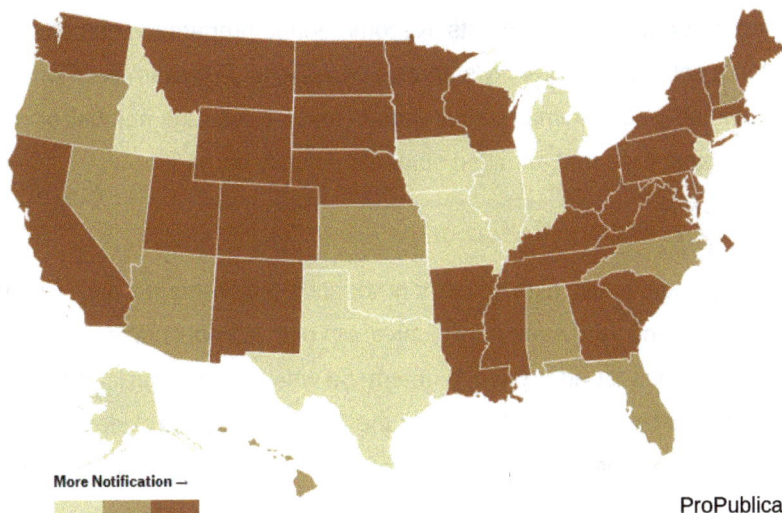

More Notification →

ProPublica

Activity 2.1: Legal Requirements of Homeschooled Students

First, research and record the legal requirements for homeschoolers in your area. Use the box below:

Second, determine your graduation requirements. Activity 2.2 will guide you. Public school graduation requirements may be set by the state, a state-designated entity, or local school districts, whereas private schools and homeschools may have control over requirements for their students. Although your student may not have to meet your local high school's graduation requirements, knowing what those requirements are helps you understand what is typical for students in your area.

In addition, admitted students at colleges and universities often exceed state minimum graduation requirements. Recommended preparation can often be found on a college or university's admission website. For example, Florida State University lists both minimum requirements and the average number of credits in each subject area that admitted students actually earned.

Activity 2.2: High School Graduation Requirements

Locate your local public high school's graduation requirements, any state-wide requirements, and your state public university high school course recommendations for admission to determine what is most applicable to your student. The Education Commission of the States website provides high school graduation requirements charts with individual state requirements and links to relevant official documents (see Resources).

Subject	State and/or local requirements	State public university recommended courses
Math		
Science		
English Language Arts		
Social Studies		
Language Other Than English		
Health & PE		
Fine Arts		
Electives		
Other		

Step 2: Think About Specific Subjects

An American high school education consists of core subject areas
supplemented with elective courses as well as health and physical education.
Although students can do interdisciplinary studies instead of learning strictly
delineated subject matter, knowing the core subject areas helps you
demonstrate how your student covered them and learned the relevant skills.

Colleges vary in the number of credits they require from the five core subjects.
Some strongly recommend that applicants complete a minimum of four credits
in each core subject; others allow for some flexibility. Using a "5 x 4" strategy
keeps the most options open. You can tailor your choices according to the
interests and aptitudes of your student. If your student follows a self-directed
path, your state's list of essential high school skills can provide a helpful
reference when you are describing what they have done.

Figure 2.2: Core Subject Areas & Options

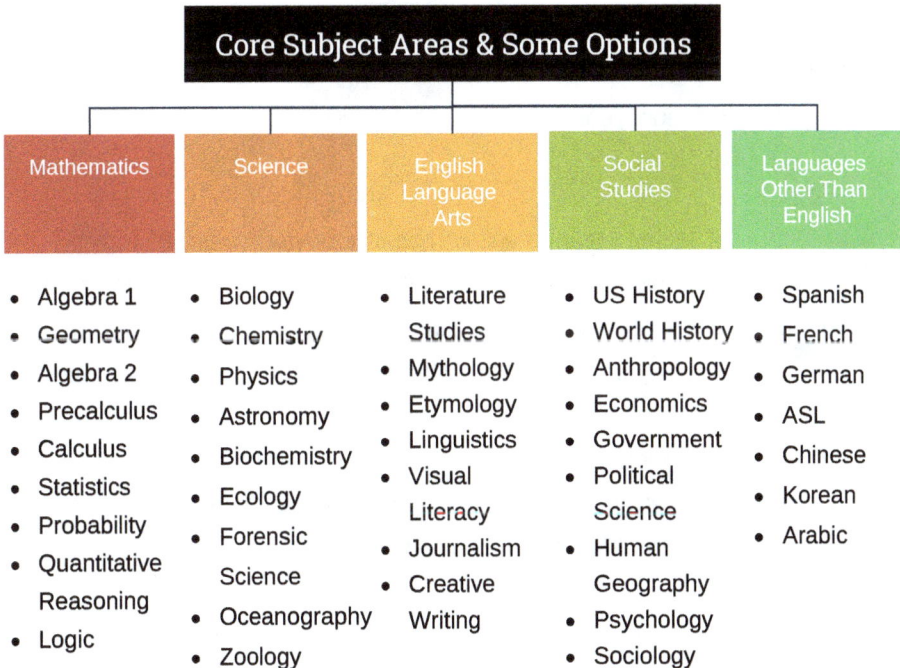

Core Subject Areas & Some Options

Mathematics	Science	English Language Arts	Social Studies	Languages Other Than English
• Algebra 1 • Geometry • Algebra 2 • Precalculus • Calculus • Statistics • Probability • Quantitative Reasoning • Logic	• Biology • Chemistry • Physics • Astronomy • Biochemistry • Ecology • Forensic Science • Oceanography • Zoology	• Literature Studies • Mythology • Etymology • Linguistics • Visual Literacy • Journalism • Creative Writing	• US History • World History • Anthropology • Economics • Government • Political Science • Human Geography • Psychology • Sociology	• Spanish • French • German • ASL • Chinese • Korean • Arabic

Mathematics

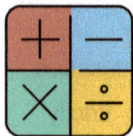

Math is perhaps the easiest subject to define. The typical cluster of high school math includes Algebra I, Geometry, Algebra II, and Precalculus. Trigonometry may be a separate course, or it may be combined with Algebra II or Precalculus. Many college-bound students complete Calculus in high school; some even go beyond.

Some high schools use an integrated high school math approach, interweaving concepts from Algebra I, Geometry, Algebra II, and Trigonometry instead of dividing algebraic from geometric concepts. The three-year sequence is commonly named Integrated Math I, II, and III. Either approach is valid.

Other courses commonly categorized as mathematics include Statistics, Probability, Quantitative Reasoning, and Logic. Depending on the content of courses on finance (such as Personal or Small Business Finance), those classes may also be included under the math umbrella.

Even if a student studied Algebra, Geometry, or more before high school, many institutions of higher education want to see four years of mathematics taken during the high school years.

Science

The three main areas of high school science are Biology, Chemistry, and Physics. Colleges commonly expect to see all three of these on a student's transcript, preferably along with a fourth year of science. Other common science classes include Earth Science, Environmental Science, and advanced classes in the primary sciences (e.g., AP Biology, AP Chemistry, and the AP Physics courses). Additional areas of science that homeschoolers can study include Astronomy, Biochemistry, Ecology, Forensic Science, Oceanography, and Zoology to name just a few.

At least two of the three primary science classes should have a lab component, and, ideally, all will. Some colleges specifically ask for formal lab reports from homeschoolers. Lab experience helps students master scientific concepts, develop scientific reasoning, and understand the complexity and ambiguity of experimental work. Whether a student is in a kitchen or a fully-equipped community college chemistry lab, they can do experiments, form hypotheses, test their hypotheses, document their work, adjust their hypotheses or procedures, and try again.

English Language Arts

Colleges expect students to take English Language Arts (ELA) courses every year of high school. Each course increases a student's literacy skills in multiple ways, and as a student matures, so does their ability to read and write about complex ideas. Homeschoolers have great latitude in how to fulfill these requirements.

Skills include reading and writing, listening and speaking, and viewing and creating visual media. Literature study incorporates writing such as short stories, novels, poetry, plays, essays, and nonfiction of varying lengths. Research techniques, source citation, literary analysis, critical thinking, identification of logical fallacies, and checking sources are all skills that improve with practice.

For ideas about content and what to learn, you can search your state's board of education site for standards by grade level. You may also find ideas for ELA electives. For example, the Tennessee State Board of Education lists many electives approved for high schools in that state, including Contemporary Literature, Japanese Mythology, Etymology & Linguistics, Visual Literacy (such as graphic novels or advertisements), Journalism, and Advanced Creative Writing.

Social Studies

High school social studies goes beyond the study of history to include a range of disciplines about human behavior, relationships, and institutions. Anthropology, Economics, Government, Political Science, Human Geography, Psychology, and Sociology all fall under the umbrella of Social Studies.

American high school students typically complete a year-long course in U.S. History and another year of World History. State requirements vary and may include state history, local history, civics, government, or even government participation.

These studies expose students to different times, cultures, and ways of thinking. Students develop critical thinking skills and apply them to complex topics and problems. They learn to communicate their thoughts clearly and with supporting evidence.

Languages Other Than English

Graduation requirements and college admission requirements vary widely when it comes to the study of a second language. Many high schools require a minimum of two consecutive years of the same non-English language. Although some colleges and universities require two or three years of language study in the same language, others recommend that applicants complete four years of high school language learning. Advanced language courses often include culture, history, and literature.

American Sign Language (ASL) often counts as a second language in high school. Families should confirm with individual colleges and universities whether ASL fulfills the college's language requirement for admission.

Physical Education and Health

Although not necessarily considered core subjects, Health and Physical Education (PE) classes are typically included in high school. PE and Health can be combined into a joint course or separated into individual courses. PE courses most often include sports, both individual and team, and personal fitness activities promoting cardiovascular endurance, strength, flexibility, and coordination. Homeschoolers can complete these as formal classes or as part of healthy daily living. Health education encompasses topics such as nutrition, fitness principles, sleep hygiene, substance abuse, sexual education, overall well-being, and mental health.

Fine Arts Electives

Art creation, appreciation, history, and performance are common types of high school arts courses. Figure 2.3 lists some common art options.

Figure 2.3: Some Art Options

Visual arts: Drawing, painting, sculpture, print-making, ceramics, pottery, photography, film and video production, digital media, and graphic design.

Performing arts: Drama, theater, acting, production, directing, musical theater, and dance.

Music: Vocal or instrumental lessons, performance, music theory, music appreciation, and ensembles such as choir, band, and orchestra.

Technology Electives

Computer science and computer programming are common technology-related electives, but many other options also exist in this space. Some technology courses overlap with music, studio arts, or other disciplines. Students can consider options such as multimedia design, digital photography, digital animation (2D or 3D), sound production, stage lighting, and video production.

Step 3: Add Unique Sizzle to Home Education

Homeschooled students need not be limited to the core high school courses or a handful of electives. For inspiration and ideas, look at college course catalogs, continuing education programs, apprenticeships, certifications, community art centers, and museum offerings.

Figure 2.4: Some Additional Sources of Unique Studies

College catalogs | Continuing ed programs | Apprentice-ships | Certifications | Community art centers | Museums

Does your child light up when speaking about or learning anything related to science but get turned off by the thought of literature or history? Their studies of language arts and social studies can be fine-tuned accordingly. Your student could read biographies of scientists, debates about the ethics of scientific choices, essays about scientific developments and their ramifications, and the history of science.

Is your child an artist and not inclined to study science? Optics is the branch of physics that studies the behavior and properties of light. Chemistry explains why gemstones have different colors, how pigments work, and the differences between acrylic and oil paints. Studying anatomy and physiology benefits portrait artists. Consider which specific topics are most related to your young person's interests; if an overview course is not appealing, look for or develop a specialty study.

What about the student who prefers hands-on activities, such as welding or blacksmithing? Experiential learning is becoming increasingly popular, and there are natural ways to connect practical skills to subjects such as science, history, and art.

Think creatively and feel free to study topics that are outside or beyond the core high school curriculum. Unique choices can develop a student's agency, interests, and maturity.

Step 4: Being Mindful of Special Considerations

You may need to take into account additional circumstances and possible requirements when making your four-year plan. For example, student athletes who want to play National Collegiate Athletic Association (NCAA) sports need to be aware of the NCAA eligibility standards.

As your student develops their Career Factor (see *College UnMazed* Chapter 3), they may find majors they would like to explore. If so, you and your student can look for ways to gain experience in and knowledge about those fields when planning high school.

Students who would like to major in particular disciplines like nursing or engineering need to be aware of common requirements such as lab sciences and possibly calculus. Those who want to study performing or studio arts may need to prepare a portfolio or audition pieces. Students with learning differences requiring accommodations need those accommodations formalized long before standardized testing. Return to your goals and your student's goals to be sure your student meets any prerequisites and is eligible and competitive in the admissions process.

Although we have been dealing with standards and requirements, these details do not need to be the sole focus of your homeschooling. You have many ways to provide an appropriate education and support your child's independence and individuality. You are not beholden to any limiting vision of how a topic must be taught. Homeschooled students often explore independently and research subjects they want to know more about. Such self-motivated learning provides delight and can also be an advantage in the college admissions process.

> **Note:** Some high schools require that students participate in community service. The Common App asks counselors, "Does your school require students to perform volunteer service?" Although service may well be one of your family values, you do not gain anything by making it an official graduation requirement. Compulsory service does not tend to carry the same weight as does volunteerism freely chosen.

Step 5: Create a Schedule and Plan

One approach to scheduling mimics a traditional high school experience by having the student study each subject daily throughout the academic year. This plan can ensure your student has the appropriate number of credits.

But what if your teen moves more quickly or slowly than expected? If your child is excited about a particular subject and masters the material rapidly, do you set that subject aside for the rest of the academic year or support them in pursuing more advanced studies? If your teen needs more time, do you stop at the end of the year and grade them based on the percentage of material they have covered to date? Your answer may vary depending on the year and the subject. We invite you to experiment to find what works well in your home.

Another approach to scheduling allows a student to focus on one subject at a time, and spend many hours a day studying it. Once the subject is mastered or a set time period ends, the student moves on to a different subject. Some colleges arrange their terms this way. For example, Colorado College uses a block plan in which students take one class for 3.5 weeks and then move on to another class.

Your homeschool can use one of these methods or a blended method that suits your student and your family. In the next chapter, we will cover a variety of sources for your homeschool studies; some of those will impact the scheduling that you choose.

Homeschool Individualized Academic Plan

Now it's time to make your own plan, taking into account all the considerations we covered. Feel free to also pencil in interdisciplinary studies or the study of subjects not typically covered in high school.

Figure 2.5 is a sample Homeschool Individualized Academic Plan to help you get started. This is not a prescription; it is one possible way to help a student meet both state requirements and college admissions requirements.

In this sample, the student completes courses in all five core subjects for all four years of high school. We assumed the student took Algebra 1 in middle school, though many students take this class during the high school years. Electives will be driven by student interest (see Step 2 for examples). After looking at the sample, use Activity 2.3 to create your own plan.

Figure 2.5: Sample Homeschool Individualized Academic Plan

Subject	#	Year 1	Year 2	Year 3	Year 4
Math	4	Geometry	Algebra 2	Pre-Calc	Calculus
Science	4	Biology	Chemistry	Physics	AP or DE science of choice
English Language Arts	4	ELA 9 (including logical fallacies)	ELA 10 (including more lit analysis)	ELA 11 (including research)	ELA 12 (genre of choice)
Social Studies	4	World History (20th cent.)	U.S. History (revolution, civil rights)	Govt., Civics	Sociology or Psychology
Language Other Than English	4	Spanish 1	Spanish 2	Spanish 3	AP or DE Spanish
Health & PE	1	Ongoing. Physical fitness (exercise principles, developing and maintaining a personal plan). Health topics as appropriate, including physical and mental wellness, nutrition, substance abuse, and human sexuality.			
Fine Arts Electives	1–2	Music lessons, performance ensembles. Museum visits with docents. Art lessons.			
Electives	2–8	Depends on interests and availability. Choose one to two each year.			

Activity 2.3: Homeschool Individualized Academic Plan

Follow these steps to create your own plan:

- **First:** List any courses that your student has already completed along with the number of credits they earned.
- **Second:** Using the work you've done earlier in this chapter, enter the target number of credits you'd like your student to earn during high school. You may list both the minimum and the preferred number of credits.
- **Third:** Complete the chart for the remaining years of high school.

Subject	#	Year 1	Year 2	Year 3	Year 4
Math					
Science					
English Language Arts					
Social Studies					

Subject	#	Year 1	Year 2	Year 3	Year 4
Language Other Than English					
Health & PE					
Fine Arts Electives					
Electives					

Summary

Congratulations! You worked through the details of the requirements and made an overall Homeschool Individualized Academic Plan to ensure that your student will have a well-rounded high school education. Next, we can think about your child as an individual learner and consider how they can meet high school requirements in ways that are meaningful to them.

CHAPTER 3
Developing and Choosing Courses

Create an Engaging Experience

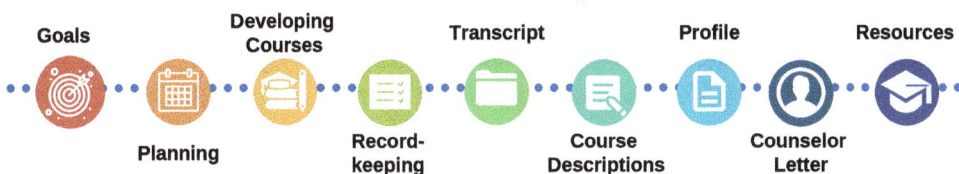

Goals · Developing Courses · Transcript · Profile · Resources

Planning · Record-keeping · Course Descriptions · Counselor Letter

In Chapter 2, you developed a plan for what your student will study and when. In this chapter, we focus on how your student will learn the material. Reflect on your teen as a learner in general and then think about how they might best learn specific topics or subjects. Methods may need to change as your child matures. To study a required subject at an introductory level, one student might learn best from short videos while another might prefer to read a book. At some point, your teen may also seek out a mentor, textbooks, recordings of college-level lectures, or a class. A preteen may need outside motivation and structure to keep on task in their learning.

As homeschooled students proceed through high school, they will likely take more responsibility for their own learning and scheduling. Sometimes, maturity brings the ability for a student to set their own pace; other times, students and parents come to understand that deadlines set by others help ensure accountability, especially for less-motivating topics.

This chapter provides an overview of many of the types of sources you can choose from when planning your child's educational path. Remember, you do not have to do this alone. In many homeschooling communities, both in person and online, parents and teens share resources and create learning experiences together. Books, websites, podcasts, conferences, and educational consultants can all assist you in this process.

To develop your coursework, you will work through five steps:

1. **Identify your priorities and parameters:** You will pinpoint considerations important to your family.
2. **Create personalized homeschool courses:** You will learn three frameworks for homeschool studies.
3. **Consider a full buffet of choices:** You will survey the variety of options available to homeschoolers.
4. **Contemplate online classes:** You will explore online classes that may fit your goals.
5. **Plan your year:** You will list courses and select among them.

Note: In this chapter, feel free to complete steps 2–4 in any order. You may need to revisit these steps throughout the high school years as your homeschooling progresses and evolves.

Step 1: Identify Your Priorities and Parameters

When making plans, keep in mind your family's priorities and any limits that you will work within, including those that arise from both necessity and choice.

Priorities may be a constant for the whole family or specific to an individual for a certain time. It is important for your family to decide what the top priorities are for each year and for each individual.

For instance, a student who is ready for college-level chemistry and wants to be in a lab with other students may want to take a community college dual enrollment chemistry class. Determining how that can be arranged, what the schedule will be, and how much it will cost impacts choices in other subjects. If that class and lab offer multiple sessions, a different opportunity that has no flexibility may be added to the schedule first.

Activity 3.1: Worksheet for Priorities and Constraints

Consider each priority listed and then write a description of each one and how it might affect your family or student. Label each category with a 1 to 5 priority rating (with 1 being the highest priority and 5 being a low priority). We have provided two additional lines if your family has a priority or constraint not listed.

Category	Description	Priority Rating
Budget		
Distance/transportation		
Technology availability		
Content to include or avoid		
Learning differences		
Health concerns		
Social concerns		
Quality/rigor of courses		
Outside rating of courses (e.g. AP designation or accredited school)		

Step 2: Create Personalized Homeschool Courses

Homeschoolers have the autonomy to design their own studies and delve deeply into topics that are particularly interesting to them. Even as you ensure your student covers material that will prepare them for college, you need not feel constrained to recreate traditional schooling in your home. You can create interdisciplinary studies, combining subjects such as history and science or literature and art. Your teen can choose to focus or broaden their studies in ways that would not be available to them in a typical high school. The educational materials and sources you select need not be limited to textbooks.

A class about U.S. History, for example, could be approached in many ways. Do you want a survey course, touching on the highlights of each decade? Would you prefer to focus on one or two time periods or topics? Either way works. Students at one co-op spent a semester of U.S. History focused on the American Revolution by using primary sources such as newspaper articles, *Common Sense* by Thomas Paine, and a selection of *The Federalist Papers*. During the second semester, some students focused on the Civil Rights movement, using primary sources and documentaries such as *Eyes on the Prize*. Other students spent second semester studying U.S. women's history, using the book *When Everything Changed* by Gail Collins as their guide.

A generative AI tool such as ChatGPT can serve as a brainstorming aid when you are planning. A well-crafted prompt will define the role, the task, and how you want the results presented. Tinker with the detail you provide in the prompt, modifying as needed (see Figure 3.1).

Figure 3.1: AI Search Prompt Example and Modifications for U.S. History

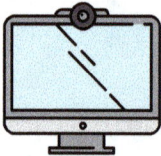

Initial prompt: You are a high school curriculum director for a homeschooled student. Design a survey course for U.S. History targeted to the 11th-grade level. Suggest a variety of primary source and secondary source materials. Include a mix of traditional and new media sources as well as projects and experiential learning opportunities. Divide the subject into nine month long units.

If the AI response has a noticeable gap, you can respond with a modification such as, "Add some primary and secondary sources written by or about women."

You can also request expansions: "Provide two additional units that would cover the period after WWII. You do not need to repeat the initial course; these are optional add-ons."

Three Course Design Options

You can approach curriculum design in a myriad of ways, but we will consider three specific approaches: preplanned, flexible planning, and organic development.

Figure 3.2: Curriculum Structure Options

Preplanned	Flexible Planning	Organic Development
• Define learning topics in advance	• Choose a subject to cover	• Recognize learning that student does naturally
• Create syllabus of assignments and tests	• Adapt activities and assessments	• Develop at own pace and depth of learning
• Follow your planned schedule	• Add resources based on interest	• Identify the subject(s) covered

Preplanned: When designing a course in advance, you can gather materials, estimate the amount of time it will take to cover concepts in appropriate depth, and then sketch out a description and schedule.

Flexible Planning: You can also prepare a general outline or starting point for a course and then invite your student to identify topics of particular interest. You will then go into depth in those areas while remaining at the survey level for others. Adapt your plans as your student discovers new sources that develop their interest in and knowledge of a subject. Their studies can be supported by a cornucopia of resources including podcasts, YouTube channels, magazines, books, documentaries, and newspaper articles. Discussing the subject with other people, including mentors, family, and friends, may lead to more in-depth explorations.

Teens often want to spend time on their interests and determine the material they will explore. This drive is a natural extension of what can be observed during infancy—that humans are curious. One Forbes 30 Under 30 educator saw his students' AP Statistics success rate skyrocket after he incorporated into the class the topics his students requested: the state basketball team's chances of winning the NBA title, voter power, online dating, and urban or rural so-called "food deserts." Flexible planning honors your student's curiosity.

Organic Development: Self-directed learning continues throughout a lifetime and may certainly be part of homeschooling high school. Initiative is an excellent trait to demonstrate to colleges and universities.

You may need to document some of your student's independent learning after it occurs. Your student might have spent significant time in a pursuit that was not planned to be a course but did end up covering all or most of the material that a class would cover. For example, a student who enjoys programming might have learned a new computer language to design a game they envisioned. A student who enjoys movies might have investigated the history of cinema, analyzed the impact of movies on culture, or learned the behind-the-scenes work involved in filming. These independent pursuits may be documented as educational experiences.

Some home educators may feel reluctant to recognize and document studies that were not planned as a "class," but it is completely valid to do so. Unique explorations can be worthwhile and academically appropriate. If you feel unsure, conduct some quick research to find if a high school or college offers a class that resembles your student's independent pursuit. You can also use such course descriptions as models for how to describe what your student has done (see also Chapter 6: Course Descriptions).

Figure 3.3 gives an example of the three course design options used for studying Geometry.

Figure 3.3: Three Possible Structures for Geometry

Preplanned: Decide in advance that the learner will use the McGraw Hill textbook along with the eStudent Edition Online and work through the first ten chapters for high school level Geometry, or all chapters if they want the course to be honors level. The student will have regular assignments and a test after each chapter.

Flexible planning: Plan for the learner to try different Geometry options including IXL Math, Khan Academy, and the McGraw Hill textbook to determine which works best for them. Once the student chooses a primary method, they may use the other options as supplementary references, especially if the explanation of a topic in their primary method isn't clear to them.

Organic development: The learner previously designed costumes and sets for a children's theater, using a variety of math skills to figure the smallest amount of materials needed in order to stretch the budget. When the student created and painted props, they calculated the area of the pieces and how much paint was required to cover them; they learned several formulas that assisted in this endeavor. As time went on, the family realized that many geometric principles were used in these projects and that the learner had covered many of the state standards for high school geometry. The student then filled in the areas that they had not yet mastered through a variety of texts and online sources. Documentation of the projects the student did, along with all the calculations made, formed a significant portion of the assessment.

Step 3: Consider a Full Buffet of Choices

Most homeschoolers take an eclectic approach to creating an educational path. You can too! The homeschool philosophy you developed in Chapter 1 will influence the resources you choose, as will your priorities, preferences, and constraints. As you decide among curricular sources (see Figure 3.4), pay attention to the mission and philosophy, both stated and unstated, of the providers you choose. How do their goals and agendas match, enrich, or challenge your own educational philosophy?

Figure 3.4: Curricular Aids and Resources

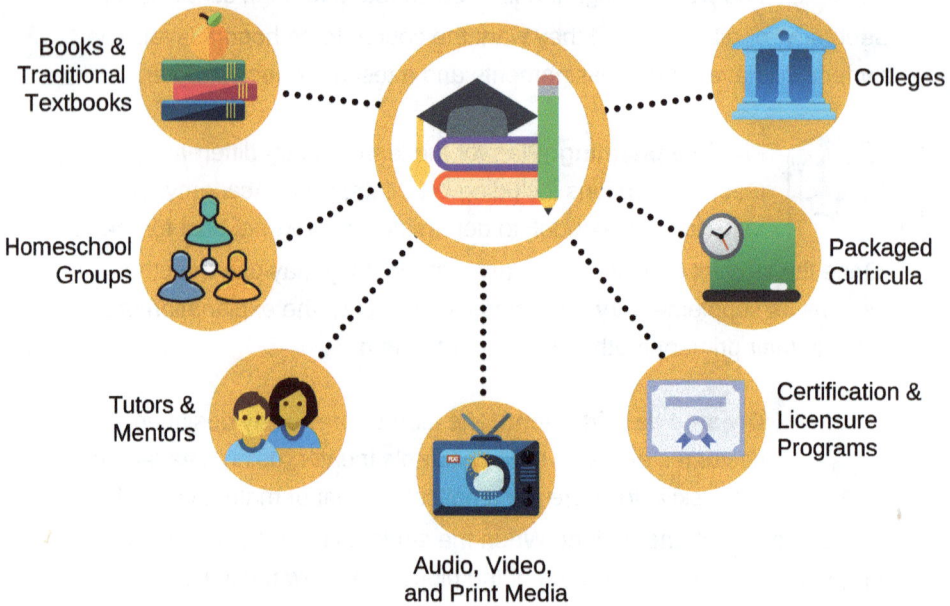

Books and Traditional Textbooks

You can use textbooks for structure or as a reference; consider teacher's guides and workbooks as well. Textbooks can also assure that you have covered the "typical content" of a course, but it is a rare textbook that entrances a teenage student. Be choosy when selecting textbooks. In her book *Cultivating Genius*, Dr. Gholdy Muhammad, Associate Professor of Literacy, Language, and Culture at University of Illinois Chicago, urges educators to reflect on both the "what" and the "how" of instruction when selecting texts.

Math is often a subject that leads homeschoolers to reach for a textbook and worksheets. There are online options as well, including adaptive systems that limit required repetition of problems that the student already mastered.

You do not need to limit yourself to standard textbooks. Consider vibrant books that can serve as a foundation or supplement for a topic that your student wants to study.

When choosing literary works, there is no need to duplicate the list a local high school requires or to focus on one world view. Literary analysis can be done with all kinds of reading material, and students are more interested in reading and writing about topics that are meaningful to them.

Some homeschooling parents share book recommendations. Amber O'Neal Johnston, a homeschooling mother who hosts local book clubs, makes her reading lists freely available on her website. In her book *A Place to Belong*, Johnston writes, "All children need books that are like mirrors in which they see themselves, as well as books that are windows into the wider world." She explains, "When we welcome their questions with expectant open arms and judgment-free, engaging dialogue, kids recognize that they have a safe space for working through their private thoughts aloud, a space where people who love them no matter what they say will guide them well."

Your homeschool resources can include a wide variety of authors who offer an equally wide variety of perspectives, thus enriching your student's experience and providing opportunities for discussions.

Homeschool Groups

Homeschooling families often seek other homeschoolers for academic and social activities, as well as for support and for sharing ideas. Homeschool groups may be organized around particular topics, activities, academic competitions, or value systems; others are multifaceted.

Homeschool cooperatives bring families together to provide students with group experiences and activities. Beyond the friendships and academic studies they provide, cooperatives can also generate leadership opportunities for students with particular interests or skills they want to share.

You can organize homeschooling groups to create field trips, Mock Trial teams, park days, group sports, and more. These groups can also involve formal study, which can be helpful when a group of students all want to learn a particular skill. You might hire an art teacher to give a drawing class to a handful of students, for example. A parent who is a chemist could lead lab activities. Language groups might gather to watch movies or have conversations in the language they are all learning; book clubs can supplement ELA courses.

You do not have to create everything from scratch; many models are already available. Try searching online. Your statewide support group may maintain a list of local groups. Look on social media as well. If you can't find what you're looking for, then reach out to other homeschooling families to see if they want to form a group with you.

Tutors and Mentors

If you work with a tutor, be sure they understand whether they are expected to follow a set curriculum and only provide additional support and explanations or if they are being engaged as the primary source of information and mentorship for a subject. Some tutors are more comfortable with the former arrangement, while others are excited to have the freedom of the latter model to personalize their sessions according to student interest.

Mentors do not need to be professional tutors; anyone with a particular interest or in a particular profession who would like to share their expertise might become a mentor for a homeschooled student.

Audio, Video, and Print Media

Pay attention to the media your student already enjoys. If you're not certain, ask your child. You might be surprised by their responses. Perhaps your student subscribes to Vsauce, Smarter Every Day, or Minute Physics and regularly watches videos on mathematical, philosophical, psychological, or scientific topics. Maybe they read magazines, or follow a favorite author who provides extensive online content including readings, appearances, and explanations about their writing process. Video series can cover a range of topics (such as TED Talks) or present more narrowly focused academic material (such as The Great Courses/Wondrium or Crash Courses). Homeschoolers can then build their own activities or projects around such series to create a full course.

Certification and Licensure Programs

Many organizations offer certification courses or apprenticeship programs. Minimum age requirements can differ by program, region, or level of license. For example, to be a licensed wildlife rehabilitator, you currently need to be 18 in Massachusetts but only 16 in New York. Some programs don't list any age requirements simply because no minors have yet asked to participate. Never hesitate to ask if a homeschooling student might be eligible to apply.

Figure 3.5: Some Certification, Training and Licensing Options

- Red Cross First Aid and CPR
- ServSafe Food Handler
- Language Proficiency
- Community Emergency Response Team (CERT)
- Certified Professional Photographer
- OSHA Safety Training Courses
- Automotive Service Excellence Student

Packaged Curricula

Some parents find it comforting to use a complete curriculum curated by an outside source. If you choose such an option, feel free to make alterations to these resources as needed. Teachers in institutional settings also make adaptations to pre-packaged curricula to fit the needs of their students, their teaching style, and their schools.

Although purchasing an individual curriculum for every class may be more expensive than purchasing an all-in-one curriculum, a piecemeal approach allows for customization. Some families find that a curriculum works well for a student for one subject, but that other subjects need a different approach.

Homeschool service providers offer a variety of materials that run the gamut from single-subject focus, like Art of Problem Solving for math, to entire universes like Ambleside Online with a Charlotte Mason focus. Some homeschool parents share or sell studies they've designed.

Colleges

Many community colleges and some four-year colleges and universities allow high school students to take college courses and earn college credit through dual enrollment or early college programs. The program names, requirements, and costs vary by location and institution. Since the classes are aimed at college students, discussion takes place at a more mature level, assignments are longer, and students are responsible for their own time management. College UnMazed offers an entire workbook (*College UnMazed: Your Guide to Dual Enrollment*) devoted to dual enrollment and the considerations that go along with this possibility.

Note: Once a student is enrolled in a college class, they are treated as an adult by that institution no matter how young they are. Students must handle themselves appropriately and be able to advocate for themselves. Parents have no role in a college class; they don't talk with professors or request adjustments to class content or dates. In addition, enrollment in a college course creates a permanent academic record. Withdrawal after the institutional deadline results in a transcript with an unexplained W.

Step 4: Contemplate Online Classes

Online classes are widely available from private teachers, companies, schools, museums, and other organizations. Some colleges offer classes online for their students and for dual-enrolled high school students. Online high schools may allow homeschooled students to enroll in single courses.

Other organizations also offer online classes to students. The Center for Talented Youth (CTY) is a nonprofit academic center of Johns Hopkins University; it offers a range of classes for advanced students. The Lukeion Project offers a variety of classes online, including Latin, Greek, Mythology, and a variety of language arts classes. Websites such as Outschool provide an abundance of classes in different lengths, formats, and levels.

Online choices also include free and subscription educational services. Khan Academy, for example, is free and provides progress reports as students move through subject tracks by watching videos, reading examples, and completing exercises. Other sites are limited to a particular subject or subject area, such as ALEKS, which focuses primarily on math.

The choices for online classes continue to expand exponentially. Other home educators may provide excellent recommendations. When selecting an online class, examine quality and content as well as how the class is conducted (see Figure 3.6) and whether students have any contact with a teacher or other students. Pay attention to the requirements of any online courses; these may include homework, group work, attendance, exams, and deadlines.

Whatever you choose, note whether it provides documentation of the learner's progress and achievements. Some online course providers will give your student a grade while others won't. Some sources may offer an official transcript while others do not. Some homeschoolers believe they should choose accredited providers, but we have not found this to be a factor in college admissions.

Figure 3.6: Online Course Structures

Asynchronous courses allow students to view materials and do assignments at any time they choose rather than having a scheduled meeting time. Some asynchronous courses require students to adhere to a pre-set schedule of assignments based on when a student begins the course, while others are completely self-paced and only require completion by the end of the term.

Synchronous courses often require students to proceed at a predetermined pace that is set by an instructor. Attendance at regularly scheduled online meetings is expected or required. Class sessions may be lecture-style or discussion-based, and students may be required to watch pre-recorded lectures on their own time. These courses often follow a typical academic calendar.

Hybrid online courses vary in their level of flexibility. They often hold fewer class meetings per week, and real-time attendance at such sessions may be optional. Recordings may be available for those students who cannot attend.

Step 5: Plan Your Year

Take this opportunity to delve deeper into creating a high school program that meets your student's needs, learning style, and family priorities. See Figure 3.7 for an example of two options for one subject. Activity 3.2 provides a place to record all your course options for the year. You can revisit this activity periodically. Use the priorities and constraints you developed in Activity 3.1 to guide your final choices.

Figure 3.7: Example of Math Plan

Subject	Source/ resources	Mode of learning	Considerations
Math: Algebra I options	Homeschool co-op	In person, with tutor and peers	• Monday afternoons • $300
	Khan Academy	Online, self-paced	• A good option if we can't meet the co-op schedule • Free

Summary

Now that you know how to develop and choose courses that fulfill your teen's goals, you can turn your attention to the records to keep and ways to evaluate student work. Chapter 4 will show you how to master this critical step. Ever onward!

Activity 3.2: Planning Your Year

Subject	Sources and resources	Mode of learning	Considerations
Math:			
Science:			
English Language Arts:			
Social Studies:			
Language Other Than English:			
Health & PE:			
Fine Arts:			
Electives:			

CHAPTER 4
Recordkeeping and Grades
Track and Assess Your Student Fairly

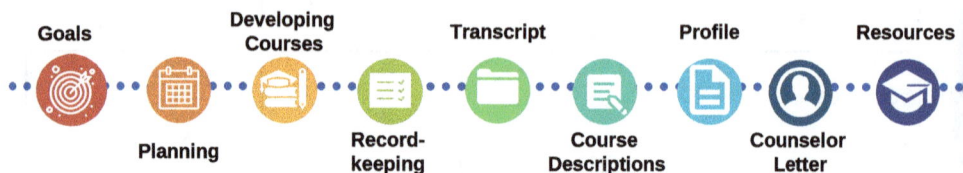

Goals   Developing Courses   Transcript   Profile   Resources

Planning   Record-keeping   Course Descriptions   Counselor Letter

You have considered requirements, how to create or choose classes, and the multiple ways your child learns. Now it is time to think about records and grades. Although some of this work can be done retroactively, keeping records and grades as you go prevents inadvertent omissions. Your records help you convey your student's accomplishments appropriately.

There are four steps to follow in this process:

1. **Collect all appropriate materials:** Determine what kinds of items to keep for your records.
2. **Assign grades and consider rubrics:** You will learn tools that can help you assess your child's work.
3. **Turn individual scores into a course grade**: You will meld multiple evaluations into a single grade.
4. **Validate academic accomplishments:** Consider options for external confirmation.

Step 1: Collect All Appropriate Materials

Homeschooling does not need to look like traditional schooling. One of the joys of homeschooling is seeing all the different ways young people engage with topics. Teens often learn outside of well-worn academic boundaries, so think broadly when maintaining proof of learning.

Although photographs and calendar entries can be sufficient documentation in the elementary years, they will not be enough on their own to produce the kind of course descriptions you need for high school. Some homeschooled teens may be interested in keeping their own records as well, especially of their more independent work. Parents are often amazed by what their own children learn and where they learn it from.

At times it's not clear whether a particular activity should be on the transcript or if it will be considered an extracurricular activity. You do not have to decide this now. Keep records as you go and determine the appropriate classification later (see Chapter 5: Transcripts).

Note: Is your child academically advanced in one or more subjects? If your student did any high school level classwork prior to 9th grade, keep those records. Otherwise, start your high school recordkeeping in the summer before 9th grade.

Figure 4.1: Gather Relevant Materials

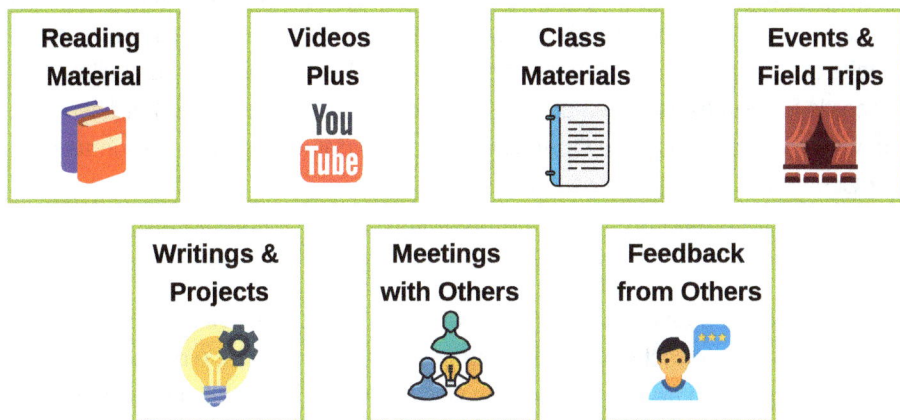

Reading Material	Videos Plus YouTube	Class Materials	Events & Field Trips

Writings & Projects	Meetings with Others	Feedback from Others

Reading Material

Keep a log of all books, graphic novels, newspapers, magazines, research journals, textbooks, blogs, and other material that your student reads, including both independent reading and any texts that were part of their defined studies. You can even include any books they read aloud to others.

Your log will include title, author, date read, and edition (if relevant). For each text or reference book, keep images of the front and back cover, publication information page, and table of contents. You can also record why your student read this material. Some students may enjoy adding notes about each item, such as who recommended it, who they talked with about it, what they learned from it, or what they agreed or disagreed with.

Videos Plus

Jot down what your teen watches or listens to, even if you are not certain it fits within any particular course. Include media such as documentaries, TV series, anime, movies, podcasts, YouTube channels, and streaming videos.

Class Materials

If your homeschooled student enrolls in a course at a school, college, or other institution that gives grades and a transcript, keep all related information: the syllabus, enrollment details like dates and teacher names, graded work, and any projects or additional work your student chooses to do. Some institutions disable access to their system after a class ends, so make sure to download all materials before you lose access. Keep similar records for non-transcripted classes that your student takes, whether from a private entity or a Massive Open Online Course (MOOC) provider such as edX or Coursera.

Events and Field Trips

Make notes on your calendar of all your child's activities. In addition to classes or scheduled learning time, be sure to include outings and field trips such as zoo or museum visits, visits to historical sites, nature hikes, park days, attendance at performances, and volunteer activities.

Writings and Projects

Save samples of what your student produces. Projects might include coding, websites, art, activities created for others, and performances. If you assign school-style homework, note the amount done and grades given. If your student loves to write, save the writing they have shared and details of how it was shared, particularly if it was submitted for publication.

Note: Some colleges ask applicants to submit writing samples, including papers submitted that received comments and/or grades from teachers.

Meetings with Others

Does your teen take music lessons? Do they garden alongside a neighbor? Do they chat regularly with an elder about what it was like to grow up before smartphones? Whether these activities are preplanned or simply serendipitous, take note because they count. You may find that such experiences supplement another study or comprise a class on their own.

Note: Mentors, teachers, or tutors that interact with a homeschooled student during their junior year could serve as recommenders during the college application process. Think ahead and create a plan that includes outside recommenders. See *College UnMazed* Chapter 7: Apply.

Feedback from Others

Keep a brag file! Whenever you receive a specific compliment or feedback about your student, save it with the date and context included. Jot down notes from verbal conversations as well. Comments from mentors, teachers, coaches, employers, and others can provide insights and quotes that you can incorporate into your counselor documentation.

Note: If a student-athlete hopes to be recruited to play a sport in college, it's important to keep records in a way that will meet NCAA requirements. The NCAA Eligibility Center publishes the NCAA Home School Toolkit to help families understand and meet their requirements.

Activity 4.1: Course Record

Use this worksheet to keep records by course title or area of study. You can customize it to fit the particular subject's characteristics. For example, you might list "Major Works Studied" when a class includes literature.

Course Record	
Facilitator or provider	
Resource(s) used	
Projects or products	
Method of assessment	
Dates	
Amount of time spent	
Additional information	

Step 2: Assign Grades and Consider Rubrics

Assigning grades to a homeschooled student can feel like a stressful process, particularly when the grades are for independent or non-traditional learning experiences. Home educators benefit from a personalized setting in which gaps in understanding tend to be noticed and addressed more quickly. Simply put, grades are not useful for evaluation to many homeschoolers. However, because traditional schools use grades to quickly sort and assess large numbers of students, colleges expect to see grades. The question isn't whether to have grades but how to represent your student's work in this form.

Just as teachers in institutional settings do not always grade every item a student produces, home educators can evaluate consistently but grade sparingly.

Note: We focus here on how to grade individualized learning experiences in the home or other non-accredited setting. In Chapter 7, we will discuss how to determine if a class should receive an Honors designation.

Many homeschooling parents opt for a mastery-based approach, which creates space and time for students to wrestle with a topic. In mastery-based learning, students revisit, revise, and reimagine with an eye toward deeper levels of discovery. Mastery-based grades tend to be high because students achieve a certain level of competency before moving on.

How do you know when your student has produced a quality response for their age or grade level? In some subject areas, this might be simple to determine. For example, you could decide that if your teen gets a 90 percent or higher on a math quiz and an 80 percent or higher on a math unit test, they know enough to tackle the next topic. Mastery doesn't have to mean perfection.

What if you also want to encourage first-time quality effort rather than potentially endless retakes? One option might be to let an original grade stand and allow for corrections at half value. Perhaps the student also needs more frequent quizzes with lower stakes.

Figure 4.2: Two Types of Grading

Traditional
- Predetermined expectations
- Scored right or wrong
- Performance measured on specific dates

Mastery Based
- Grade based on demonstration of competency
- Values improvement over time
- Multiple attempts encouraged

Although an objective standard tends to work well for subjects with right and wrong answers, how do you handle more subjective subjects? As a home educator, you get to decide what success looks like for your student. How do you evaluate your student's level of learning? Rubrics help answer this question.

According to Cornell's Center for Teaching Innovation, "A rubric is a type of scoring guide that assesses and articulates specific components and expectations for an assignment." Packaged curricula usually come with assessment rubrics. Likewise, the College Board AP Central's Course & Exam Pages provide detailed rubrics for each AP exam.

If you create your own courses, you may find grading rubrics online to suit your purposes. The free Rubistar website allows teachers to adapt customizable templates. Rubrics can be used to evaluate oral communication, written communication, teamwork, critical thinking, and much more (see Resources for more free downloadable rubrics).

AI tools can be another time-saving way to draft rubrics. Provide a clear prompt that defines the role, gives specifics about the task, and details how you want AI to produce the results (see Figure 4.3).

Figure 4.3: Rubric Example Using AI

Following Cornell's recommended guidelines for effective rubrics, you could submit the following prompt to Google Gemini or another generative AI:

Your role is as a high school curriculum developer. Create a rubric to evaluate poetry written by a 10th-grade student. The rubric should create an evaluative range for performance quality under each element; for instance, "excellent," "good," "unsatisfactory." Add descriptors that qualify each level of performance. Avoid using subjective or vague criteria such as "interesting" or "creative." Instead, outline objective indicators that would fall under these categories. The criteria must clearly differentiate one performance level from another. Assign a numerical scale to each level. Include four to five criteria and present the rubric in a chart form.

We used the prompt in Figure 4.3 and then asked Gemini to simplify the rubric to three grading columns. The results are shown in Figure 4.4.

Figure 4.4: Rubric created by Google's AI Gemini

Criteria	Excellent (3 pts)	Good (2 pts)	Unsatisfactory (1 pt)
Content & Theme	Clear and engaging theme with depth and complexity. Demonstrates original perspective or insight.	Identifies a theme, but lacks development or elaboration.	Theme is unclear or absent.
Figurative Language & Imagery	Vivid and precise use of figurative language to create powerful imagery.	Uses some figurative language, but it may be generic or unclear.	Figurative language is absent or misused.
Structure & Form	Demonstrates deliberate choice and mastery of a specific form (free verse, sonnet, haiku, etc.) or uses an innovative structure.	Uses a recognizable form, but may not fully understand its conventions.	Form is unclear or inappropriate for the chosen content.
Word Choice & Voice	Strong diction with precise word choices that paint vivid pictures and evoke emotions.	Word choice is generally clear, but may lack specificity or originality.	Word choice is vague or imprecise.
Mechanics & Conventions	Consistent and correct use of grammar, punctuation, and spelling.	Minor errors in grammar, punctuation, or spelling may occur.	Multiple errors in mechanics and conventions hinder comprehension.

Grading Scale from Gemini:

- 12-15 points: A
- 9-11 points: B
- 6-8 points: C
- 3-5 points: D
- 0-2 points: F

Another benefit of rubrics is that your student may collaborate with you in determining the criteria to use when evaluating their project or activity. Students can also use rubrics as a self-evaluation tool to reflect on their own learning progress.

When evaluating student work, value progress over perfection. Encountering challenges builds students' skills for the future. Overwhelming frustration indicates a time to regroup, set work aside, or move to something different.

Step 3: Turn Individual Scores into a Course Grade

Once you have scores for individual assignments, you need to combine them into a single overall class grade. Different types of assignments should account for a different proportion of the grade. For example, quizzes might count toward 10 percent of the final grade, while projects may contribute 50 percent. Prepackaged courses often suggest specific percentages for categories of assignments. If you adjust the materials in the prepackaged courses to suit your student's needs, you can easily adjust the percentages.

For learning experiences you design at home, you have to decide how much value each assignment carries. Remember that class grades in public and private schools are not limited to scores on tests and quizzes; homework, projects, essays, discussion, and participation can all play a role. The activities you deem most important will determine the bulk of the course grade (see Figure 4.4). If spirited discussion plays an important role in a course, give discussion a higher percentage of the overall grade. In a science class, on the other hand, you may decide that lab reports should comprise a greater share of the final grade. See additional examples of how to determine course grades in Chapter 6: Course Descriptions.

Figure 4.5: Some Products and Activities That May Be Graded

Tests & Quizzes   Homework   Projects   Essays   Discussions   Participation

Step 4: Validating Academic Accomplishments

How will colleges know whether your grades correspond to a recognized standard? You can include some forms of external assessment sprinkled through the core subject areas. This validation might consist of a graded online course, a dual enrollment course, a standardized test, or a written assessment by a tutor or mentor other than a family member.

A tangible, shareable work product by your student can also serve as evidence of their learning. Some examples of final projects that demonstrate accomplishment are a research paper, a recorded presentation, a programming project, or artistic work.

Note: Homeschooled students enrolled in classes offered by a college or online school generally receive a record and grade from that institution. Those grades are official and need to be incorporated into your records as is.

Activity 4.2: Validation per Subject Area

Use the chart on the next page to brainstorm outside evidence or assessments that demonstrate your student's level of mastery.

Summary

After keeping clear records, evaluating and grading student work, and providing some objective validation, you are ready to create counselor documents for colleges and universities to evaluate. Let's move on to Section 2, which shows you how to accurately represent your homeschool through your transcript, course descriptions, homeschool profile, and counselor recommendation.

Activity 4.2: Validation per Subject Area

Subject	Outside Validation or Tangible Work Product
Math	
Science	
English Language Arts	
Social Studies	
Language Other Than English	
Elective	

INTRODUCTION TO SECTION 2

Home educators wear many hats. In the first half of this book, you developed your role as high school planner and facilitator of an individualized educational path for your student.

In the next section of this workbook, attention turns to what colleges expect to see in application materials. You will lean into your role as documentarian and marketer as you create four core documents: transcript, course descriptions, homeschool profile, and counselor letter of recommendation. These documents must accurately reflect your student's educational journey and can add luster and sparkle to their college application.

Figure Intro 2.1: Homeschool Document Mindmap

A Word about the Timeline

We recommend that home educators begin keeping records and course documents when high school work begins. By updating your records each semester, you minimize the chance of forgetting important learning activities.

You can wait a bit before composing the homeschool profile and counselor recommendation. Parents typically write these documents during the summer before their student's senior year. This timing corresponds with when your child is likely to begin their college applications. By working in tandem, you will notice any information on the student side of the application that needs to be explained or contextualized in the counselor documents.

It is worth noting that not every college or university requires all four documents from every homeschooled applicant. However, college lists often shift as families refine their Six Keys of College Fit: Academic Match, Career Match, Financial Match, Personal Match, Student Outcomes, and Student Support (see *College UnMazed* for more information). If you create each of the four core homeschool counselor documents, you can meet any school's particular application requirements for homeschooled applicants.

When you have completed the four core documents, you are ready to submit them to colleges. Various application platforms ask for and allow different uploads. Always follow the instructions for the particular platform and reach out to the admissions office when in doubt. If a college or university offers multiple ways to apply, they usually do not have any preference about which method a student chooses.

Crafting quality documents helps you advance along the timeline for success. Let's move on and learn how to create each document you'll need to substantiate your student's high school experience.

Figure Intro 2.2: A Timeline for Success

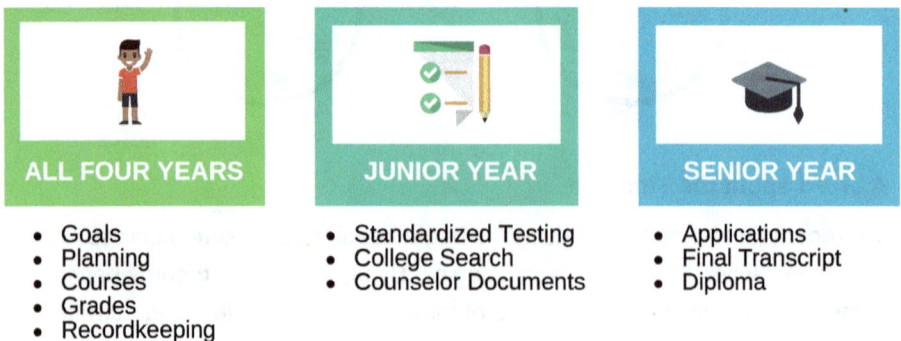

ALL FOUR YEARS
- Goals
- Planning
- Courses
- Grades
- Recordkeeping

JUNIOR YEAR
- Standardized Testing
- College Search
- Counselor Documents

SENIOR YEAR
- Applications
- Final Transcript
- Diploma

CHAPTER 5
Transcript

Showcase Your Teen's Learning Concisely

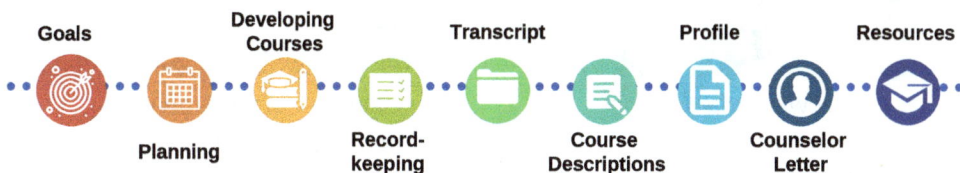

Goals · Developing Courses · Transcript · Profile · Resources

Planning · Record-keeping · Course Descriptions · Counselor Letter

In this chapter, you will learn how to create an accurate transcript that concisely reflects your student's high school education. You will discover what makes an effective transcript and how to produce a document that provides admission readers with an at-a-glance understanding of your student's record.

The best time to create a transcript is before your student starts applying to colleges or other official programs. Even if a college does not request a transcript during the application process, they will require your student's final official transcript prior to enrollment. Your student also may be asked to self-report their academic record in a format determined by the college. Having the transcript available ensures consistent and accurate reporting.

You will follow four steps to generate a transcript:
1. **Decide on the format:** You will decide whether a transcript organized by year or by subject makes the most sense for your homeschooler.
2. **Determine placement:** You will decide whether an experience belongs on the transcript or in the activities list.
3. **Include essential information:** You will include required items in a clear way.
4. **Calculate the GPA:** You will discover the pros and cons of weighted and unweighted GPAs.

Step 1: Decide on the Format

Transcripts can be organized either by high school year or by subject area. Neither option is inherently better than the other, and each has advantages (see Figure 5.1).

Figure 5.1: Transcript Organization Options

By High School Years	By Subject Area
• Follow standard school calendar • Shows year-over-year grade trends • Appropriate if core subjects are completed every year	• Can reflect year-round or non-traditional calendars • Shows grade trends by subject • Showcases areas of depth

A transcript **formatted by year** makes it easy for readers to note grade trends and detect whether the overall difficulty level of their course load increased as the student proceeded through high school. A transcript formatted by year might also show that your student was more academically successful as high school progressed. Transcripts organized by year tend to work well for students who follow the standard school calendar, take courses from the full range of core subjects each year, and begin and end those courses during a single academic year. This style of transcript also provides an easy way to showcase the student's GPA each year as well as their cumulative GPA.

Transcripts **formatted by subject** highlight extra or in-depth study done in one or more academic disciplines and show increasing rigor in particular areas. A subject transcript calls attention to "pointy" areas of interest. This format may be a strong choice for those with multiple interests outside of core subjects because electives can be subdivided into specific categories. A subject-formatted transcript can be a good choice if your student's high school spanned five years due to student illness or for other reasons. Additionally, not all homeschoolers follow a traditional school year calendar. Some studies might last six weeks while others might take place over multiple years. A subject transcript accurately portrays those classes.

Pick the format that best suits the strengths of your homeschool choices.

Step 2: Determine Placement

Sometimes it can be difficult to decide whether a significant endeavor should be transcripted as a class or whether that learning should be recorded as an activity. Literature clubs that form a component of a student's language arts learning, music instruction, or an apprenticeship could work in either spot. Hands-on learning, particularly within an informal group of friends, often blurs the line between a class and an extracurricular activity.

First, look at your transcript. Does the experience round out an area where the student may be light on credits? If so, think about what your student produced or how they demonstrated their learning in a way that could be worth awarding credit. Perhaps the student annotated a novel and led a Socratic discussion of essential questions with a group of peers. Maybe they completed an apprenticeship requiring knowledge of how their local government works. If the material learned was significant enough for at least a half credit, consider recording the experience as a course.

Second, decide where the experience would shine brightest. Some home educators are eager to make everything into a credit because they have not yet examined the different sections of a college application. It is easy for an experience to get lost in a sea of credits. Perhaps that same activity will sparkle as one of a student's listed extracurriculars.

Finally, be unique rather than strange. If an institutionally-schooled student would likely place an activity as an extracurricular, it may make sense for your student to follow suit. Does the placement of an educational activity in the student activity list or on the transcript raise questions or answer questions? Admission officers want to understand why you made the choices you did. If you opt for an unusual placement, explain your rationale. Course descriptions, covered in our next chapter, offer one such opportunity for elaboration. Figure 5.2 provides examples of two different transcript decisions parents could make about the same educational activity.

Figure 5.2: Two Different Transcript Decisions for Science Olympiad

Jaden studied Biology at home in grade 9. In grade 10, he took AP Environmental Science from an online provider, and did Science Olympiad. In grades 11 and 12, he completed introductory courses in Chemistry and Physics at the four-year regional college.

Jaden's 10th grade Science Olympiad events included Forestry, Wind Power, and Experimental Design. Jaden listed this experience in his Activities List on his application.

Min followed delight-driven, student-selected learning in grades 9 and 10. In grade nine, she completed Ferret Ecology, a problem-based learning biology curriculum. In grade 10, she participated in the Science Olympiad in Forestry, Wind Power, and Experimental Design. In grades 11 and 12, she completed introductory courses in Chemistry and Physics at a four-year regional college.

Min listed her Science Olympiad learning as a credit on her transcript for grade 10 as Wood, Wind, and Wisdom: Observation & Experimentation. Her parent wrote a detailed course description including all the resources Min consulted during her sophomore year. Min listed her regional Science Olympiad awards in the Honors/Awards portion of her college application.

Step 3: Include Essential Information

What makes a transcript official? The simplest answer is that it must say "Official High School Transcript" and be signed by the homeschooling parent or guardian. In most cases, there is no need to notarize or place a seal on the transcript.

Figure 5.3: Information Included on Transcripts

| Student Information | Start & Grad Date | Credits | GPA & Weighting | Credit Hour | Signature & Statement |

Transcripts include the following:
- Your student's legal name, birth date, and address
- The start date and the planned graduation date
- The total number of credits earned to date and expected by graduation
- The grading scale, GPA, and an explanation of any weighting
- Your definition of a credit hour
- Your signature, with the date, under a line such as "I, [parent name], Homeschool Advisor for [student name], certify that the above courses and grades are an accurate reflection of [their] work, and that homeschooling was done in accordance with the laws of [state]."

Figure 5.4: Information Included for Each Class on the Transcript

Course Name → Subject & Year → Course Level → Number of Credits → Grade Earned → Source of Course

For each class, indicate:
- The course name
- The subject area and the year taken
- The course level (e.g., college prep, honors, AP, college)
- The grade earned or a note if the course is in progress or planned for future semester
- The number of credits awarded for the course
- The source of the course (optional)

Note: Most institutions accept a homeschooled student's parent-issued final transcript as official proof of graduation. A few schools place an extra burden on homeschoolers. As always, check with the individual college or university for their application and enrollment requirements.

For example, the University of Massachusetts Amherst requires admitted homeschooled students "to provide the university with proof of graduation in one of the following ways:
- An official final transcript from the local school district.
- An official final transcript from a home-school association or agency.

- An official GED/HiSET score report.
- An official college transcript(s) showing successful completion of 27 college credits."

If a college requires documentation that your own state law does not support or allow, reach out to the college or university. They may be unaware of how homeschooling works in your state.

As you list classes on your student's transcript, include all courses from outside providers, any dual enrollment classes, and any home-created courses. Be sure your course title matches the one given by any institution that creates an official record that colleges may want to see. Some students begin homeschooling later in high school after attending a brick-and-mortar school. Classes from the previous public or private school are generally listed on the comprehensive homeschool transcript exactly as they appear on the school transcript.

Many homeschoolers today take classes from a variety of public and private providers. This practice is sometimes referred to as "flexi-schooling." If your teen's classes come from a variety of sources, list the source of the class after the title or footnote it.

Sometimes a student repeats a class to improve their understanding and grade. You need to determine your policy for repeated classes. Will both grades remain on the transcript and be included in the GPA? Will the repeated grade replace the original grade in GPA calculations? How will you show the repeated class on the transcript? Whatever you decide, clearly articulate your decisions about repeated classes in your homeschool profile (see Chapter 7).

Some homeschools issue semester grades; others only issue grades at course completion. This choice is a matter of personal preference based on the mix of courses chosen. Similarly, either letter or number grades work equally well as long as you provide a grading scale. The conversion can be tricky when you're working with multiple providers and they have different grading scales. You might pick the most common scale for your master transcript and add the explanatory phrase "dependent upon provider." You can unpack the various grading methodologies in your homeschool profile.

Admission readers will want to know how your homeschool defines a credit hour. Credits can be defined on your transcript by including a statement such as "1 credit hour = 120 hours or a one-term dual-enrolled college class." We recommend one credit for classes that covered the same material as a standard high school course, even if you condense or expand the time allotted to complete that class. Be aware that college classes can vary in the amount of credit the college awards, especially for classes with lab components. We suggest any one-term college class receive one credit on the high school transcript.

Your transcript will include a graduation date. For student-athletes hoping to participate in college athletics, it is important to also include a start date for ninth grade. Some home educators also like to include the minimum number of credits required for graduation from their homeschool in addition to the actual number of credits earned.

Note: Today, many colleges and universities don't require test scores for admission. In the past, some transcripts included standardized test scores. The test-optional landscape is tricky to navigate, and best practices have shifted toward leaving standardized test scores off transcripts.

Unless your student knows that their test scores enhance their application at every institution to which they are applying, do not include their test scores on the transcript. There are other places on a college application where a student can choose to include this information.

Step 4: Calculate GPA

Admission officers need to understand your student's GPA in context, so decide whether to use a weighted GPA, an unweighted GPA, or both. Weighted GPAs often give a boost of +0.5 for Honors courses and +1 for Advanced Placement, International Baccalaureate, and college classes taken through dual enrollment. An unweighted GPA does not provide a multiplier for advanced courses. Many times, a transcript will include both a weighted and unweighted GPA, both by year and cumulatively for the high school career.

The 4.0 grading scale is generally considered the most common. If weighted grades are used, it's possible for a student to have a GPA higher than a 4.0. Many public and private school students also show similarly high GPAs. Some colleges and universities accept whatever GPA is on the transcript, so it makes sense to report the highest ethically-determined GPA. The Resource section of this book includes a link to a GPA calculator that computes both weighted and unweighted grades.

Note: Many colleges and universities recalculate each applicant's GPA with an institution-specific method. One typical formula counts only core subjects, omitting electives.

If your student took more than four credits of classes from a core area, you may be tempted to list the "extra" courses as electives. We recommend grouping them with their core subject area instead.

If your student earned high school credit prior to ninth grade, you may include those classes on the homeschool transcript. Math and languages other than English represent the most common sorts of high school credits earned in middle schools, but homeschooled students may be accelerated in other subject areas as well. Some people opt to include these classes in the high school GPA; others decide to count the credit but not the grade. Either way works, provided you include a note clarifying your choice.

Figure 5.5: One Common Grading Scale

Letter Grade	100 pt. scale	Unweighted	+.5 Honors	+1 AP/IB/DE
A	90-100	4.0	4.5	5.0
B	80-89	3.0	3.5	4.0
C	70-79	2.0	2.5	3.0
D	65-69	1.0	1.5	2.0

You can find samples of transcripts formatted by year linked in the Resources section of this book. Figure 5.6 on the next page gives an example of one option for a subject-formatted transcript. Notice how this transcript includes the elements listed in Step 3 of this chapter.

Summary

A transcript conveys your student's academic journey in a single page. It should provide compelling evidence of why an admissions committee should say yes to your student. Next, you will turn to course descriptions to provide more detail about your curricular choices.

Figure 5.6: Homeschool Subject-Formatted Transcript Example

LASTNAME HOME SCHOOL
OFFICIAL HIGH SCHOOL TRANSCRIPT FOR FIRST M. LASTNAME

STUDENT INFORMATION

RECORD OF: FIRST M. LASTNAME	LASTNAME HOME SCHOOL
BIRTH DATE: mm/dd/yy	ADDRESS:
PHONE:	PHONE:
E-MAIL:	EMAIL:

CREDITS AND DATES

CREDITS COMPLETED AS OF [date - end of Junior year]: 22
TOTAL CREDITS EXPECTED BY GRADUATION: 28.5
OVERALL GPA (UNWEIGHTED): __
OVERALL GPA (WEIGHTED): __
START DATE - GRADUATION DATE: [mm/dd/yy] - [mm/dd/yy]

MATHEMATICS — CREDITS: 3.5 (4.5)

Course Title	Grade	Credit	Level	School/Source	Year
Algebra		1	Honors	Khan	9
Geometry		1	Honors	ALEKS	10
Algebra II w/Trigonometry		1	Honors	ALEKS	11
Personal Finance		.5	High S.	Coop	11
Precalculus	*	1	Honors	ALEKS	12

LANGUAGE, LITERATURE, AND COMMUNICATION — CREDITS: 3 (4)

Course Title	Grade	Credit	Level	School/Source	Year
English Comp & Lit I		1	Honors	Private	9
English Comp & Lit II		1	Honors	Private	10
English Comp & Lit III		1	Honors	Private	11
English Comp & Lit IV	*	1	Honors	Private	12

SCIENCE — CREDITS: 3 (4)

Course Title	Grade	Credit	Level	School/Source	Year
Environmental Science		.5	Honors	Coop	9
Forensic Science		.5	Honors	Coop	9
Biology w/Lab		1	Honors	Coop	10
Chemistry w/Lab		1	College	LCC	11
Physics w/Lab	*	1	College	LCC	12

HISTORY AND SOCIAL STUDIES — CREDITS: 3 (4)

Course Title	Grade	Credit	Level	School/Source	Year
World History		1	High S.	Coop	9
US History: Revolutions		.5	Honors	Coop	10
US Women's History		.5	Honors	Coop	10
US History: Civil Rights		.5	Honors	Coop	11
AP Government		.5	AP	AHS	11
Psychology	*	1	College	LCC	12

TECHNOLOGY — CREDITS: 2

Course Title	Grade	Credit	Level	School/Source	Year
Programming in Python		1	Honors	Private	10
Intro. Computer Science		1	College	edX CS50x	11

LANGUAGE OTHER THAN ENGLISH — CREDITS: 3 (4)

Course Title	Grade	Credit	Level	School/Source	Year
Japanese I		1		Private	9
Japanese II		1		Private	10
Japanese III w/Culture		1		Private	11
Japanese IV w/History	*	1		Private	12

ARTS & MUSIC — CREDITS: 1.5 (2)

Course Title	Grade	Credit	Level	School/Source	Year
Violin Performance		.5	High S.	Private	9
Violin Performance		.5	High S.	Private	10
Violin Performance		.5	High S.	Private	11
Violin Performance	*	.5	High S.	Private	12

HEALTH AND FITNESS

Course Title	Grade	Credit	Level	School/Source	Year
Health & Fitness I		.5	High S.	Private	9
Health & Fitness II		.5	High S.	Private	10
Health & Fitness III		.5	High S.	Private	11
Health & Fitness IV	*	.5	High S.	Private	12

SCHOOLS AND SOURCES

LCC = Local Community College
AHS = A____ High School
Coop = Y____ Homeschool Cooperative
Khan = Khan Academy
ALEKS = ALEKS.com mathematics courseware
Private = privately designed, including private instruction

* Course to be completed in senior year; credit not yet awarded. Total credits expected shown in ().

HOMESCHOOL CREDITS AND GRADING

Level of homeschooling courses determined by homeschool director and instructors, taking into account the textbooks and digital resources used, understanding required, and assigned workload. Determination of grades dependent on provider. See Course Descriptions (attached) for details.

1 credit = equivalent of 120 hours of work, or one college course.

Grades: A 4.0, A- 3.7, B+ 3.3, B 3.0, B- 2.7, C+ 2.3
GPA weight : +1 for AP/college class, +.5 for Honors

SUPERVISOR CERTIFICATION

I, [Parentfirst Parentlastname], Homeschool Director for [First M. Lastname], certify that the above courses, grades and scores are an accurate reflection of their work and that homeschooling was done in accordance with the laws of [state].

Parentfirstname Parentlastname

Parentfirstname Parentlastname
Telephone: ____ Email: ____

CHAPTER 6
Course Descriptions
Enhance Your Student's Application with Details

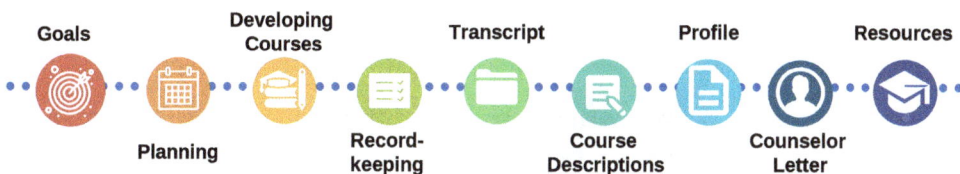

Goals | Developing Courses | Transcript | Profile | Resources
Planning | Record-keeping | Course Descriptions | Counselor Letter

In this chapter, you will learn how to strengthen your student's transcript by backing it with concise and compelling course descriptions. You will discover what makes an effective course description and how course descriptions help colleges understand the work your student completed.

Many home educators feel conflicted about what to include in course descriptions. You may be tempted to provide long descriptions of every study, but a document with exhaustive listings of commonly understood studies might get skimmed and its unique elements overlooked.

Course descriptions that actually get read bolster the student's application. They provide additional information for an admissions officer to evaluate your student. When properly done, course descriptions establish the rigor of your course offerings. An admissions representative will notice if above grade-level materials were used or if a project yielded in-depth results.

In addition to answering any questions that may arise from the transcript, course descriptions showcase the uniqueness of your homeschool journey. Your homeschooler's interests and curiosity will shine in well-written course descriptions.

To write an effective course description, you will follow these four steps:

1. **Select the appropriate information:** You will learn what key information should be included in a course description.
2. **Determine a template:** You will decide how to clearly present the information to admission readers.
3. **Personalize course descriptions:** You will personalize course descriptions to highlight student achievement.
4. **Document nontraditional courses:** You will accurately relate interest-driven and student-led learning.

Step 1: Select the Appropriate Information

For each description, you will note who provided instruction and whether the course was from a provider outside the home, was home-based, or combined elements from multiple sources. Include key resources that your student used.

Admission readers also want to know if the class met in person or online, if the course was synchronous or self-paced, and how frequently the class met.

Refer to what you developed in Activity 4.1. What method of learning did you use? How did the student demonstrate what they learned and how did you determine the grade for this class? Record the blend of learning activities, which could include projects, quizzes, tests, essays, oral presentations, artistic works, certifications gained, etc. It can be helpful to note what percentage each element contributed to the overall grade, especially for home-based courses.

Step 2: Determine a Template

To write effective course descriptions, be strategic, be brief, and be consistent.

Be Strategic. As you consider course descriptions, anticipate what admission officers might be curious about. If the order of course descriptions does not match that of your transcript, make a note at the beginning of the document about its organization. This can be as simple as, "Courses are listed by subject area, with the most recent studies listed first."

Be Brief. Admission officers are busy people. Two-person admission teams at the University of Pennsylvania, for example, read up to fifteen applications an hour. Many colleges and universities operate similarly. If your student's entire application and supporting counselor documents receive only between four and seven minutes of total review, you want readers to find what they need quickly. Be concise.

Unique or individually designed classes need additional explanation, whereas standard courses like Algebra may only require one sentence. If your student took four years of a language other than English, and the course goals, methods, and material were similar each year, consider writing one combined description for Levels 1–4, using the materials section to differentiate among levels (see Figure 6.2).

Include only the most important details for each course. If a student took an AP exam and scored a 4 or a 5, that might be worth including in the corresponding course description, especially if that was part of how you determined the course grade.

Be consistent. Following the same format for each entry gives visual cues to admission readers who are searching quickly for answers to questions they have. A sudden change of order can confuse readers. Decide what template works the best to showcase your student's abilities and then stick with that template throughout.

Figure 6.1: Considerations for Descriptions

Be Strategic	Be Brief	Be Consistent
Emphasize student's key strengths.	Keep descriptions short & concise.	Follow the same format for each entry to give visual cues.

Once you've written your descriptions, you will compile them into a single document. Some home educators include every class in this document. Others choose not to include full descriptions for dual enrollment classes or classes taken through a school that provides a transcript (see Figure 6.3). Whatever you decide, label your document accordingly and provide an introductory note. For example, "This select course description list does not detail dual enrollment classes or courses taken at XYZ High School" or "This program of studies includes all classes taken and course descriptions of private or independent studies. Courses taken from accredited institutions are listed with the date taken for reference."

Figure 6.2: Sample Description for a Repeating Class with Similar Material at Progressive Levels

---

French 1-4 (Grades 9-12, 4 credits)

Instructor: Francine Francophile, a native French speaker

Mode/Frequency: Live, online group class with 6 participants, 2x/week for 36 weeks/yr.

Description: Student acquired an awareness of Francophone cultures and basic French communication skills necessary for daily life. Students developed listening, speaking, writing, and aural comprehension skills at increasingly challenging levels. Students learned basic grammar structure and vocabulary and progressed to an advanced level, including reading literature in French.

Course materials:
Bon Voyage 1–4, McGraw-Hill
Le Petit Prince by Antoine de Saint-Exupéry
L'Étranger by Albert Camus
Guest speakers
YouTube videos of native speakers

Evaluation criteria: 15% workbook pages, 10% audio pages, 20% chapter quizzes & listening tests, 25% chapter tests, 30% writing assignments & speaking tests.

Figure 6.3: Sample Description of an External Class That Also Appears on Another Official Transcript

College Biology (Grade 10, 1 credit)
XYZ Community College course number BIO 131, Spring 2024.

Step 3: Personalize Course Descriptions

A personalized description will showcase your student's particular achievements. A class that incorporates unique features may have a bit longer description than other courses. Let's consider the example of a home-designed social studies course for Nathan, a homeschooler who wanted to study at a university that would encourage his artistic and design talents.

Throughout high school, Nathan learned in a variety of ways. He took dual enrollment college classes, homeschool co-op classes, and classes conducted in the home with siblings. He also bundled shorter academic experiences to form full credit classes. His core courses included significant opportunities for artistic expression and hands-on activities. Nathan's World Geography class exemplified this blend of academic and artistic endeavors.

Figure 6.4: Nathan's Home-Designed Social Studies Course Description

World Geography (Grade 9, 2 Semesters, 1 Credit, Grade: A)
Instructor: *Parent Name*
Mode/Frequency: Daily, in-person, in-home instruction with his two siblings.
Description: Student examined problems within cartography, surveyed the history of exploration and colonialism, and engaged in geography drawing lessons and activities to memorize world geographic features. This course moved chronologically through time as it moved

geographically through regions. Student replicated freehand from memory a detailed world map with country borders, capital cities, mountain ranges, oceans, seas, major lakes, and rivers as a culminating final project.

Course materials: *Mapping the World* by Art by Johnston and *Mapping the World by Heart* by Smith, both of which incorporated detailed geographic features and atlas work. Supplemental readings included *Longitude* by Sobel and *Guns, Germs, and Steel* by Diamond.

Evaluation criteria: 50% final project, 25% discussion, and 25% daily written responses, sketches, and hands-on projects such as creating a sextant (an instrument with a graduated arc of 60° and a sighting mechanism used for measuring the angular distances between objects and for taking altitudes in navigation).

Step 4: Document Nontraditional Courses

Course descriptions can be straightforward when the class fits a traditional model with defined parameters. What about classes in which home educators "plan from behind" and learning unfolds in a student-driven way? Unschoolers and other delight-driven learners also benefit from formalizing their experience with a course description.

How do you explain something so organic? Perusing high school or college course catalogs might be inspiring. Another option is to look at your state's grade and subject standards for listed topics and skills.

AI tools can also help you create descriptions. Perhaps your child is a theater enthusiast who demonstrated deep analysis in conversation or through writing after attending several theatrical shows. Free AI tools like Subject Explorer can generate ideas to define that experience as well as provide next steps to extend learning if needed. Some of the results such a tool produces (see Figure 6.5) could be incorporated into a course description.

Figure 6.5: AI-Generated Learning Description from Subject Explorer

---

Description/Prompt: My student attended the musicals *Hamilton, West Side Story, Come from Away, Hadestown*, and *Rent*.

Results:
- Explored the use of language in musical theater
- Examined the themes and motifs present in each play
- Analyzed the character development and relationships in each play
- Studied the historical and cultural context of each play
- Practiced critical thinking and interpretation skills through discussion and reflection

Continued development could include writing a comparative analysis of two of the plays, creating a character analysis project, or exploring the use of music and lyrics in storytelling.

Smaller related experiences can be combined to create a half or full credit. This bundling can cover several years with course credit typically awarded in the year your student completed the activities. For instance, perhaps your science-loving teen volunteered on an organic farm and learned how to keep pests at bay naturally. That, in turn, led to a deep dive into soil ecology with your child reading *The Soil Will Save Us* by Ohlson, *The Farm as Ecosystem* by Brunetti, and *Soil* by Evans. That reading prompted a kayak trip along local waterways to observe how farming methods contribute to or prevent river pollution. Finally, your student opted to create their own small garden.

Those experiences can be rolled into a one-credit class (see Figure 6.6). Another option is to highlight these choices in the Activities List portion of the college application (see Chapter 5: Transcripts).

Figure 6.6: Field Ecology Sample Course Description

Field Ecology (11–12, 4 semesters, 1 credit, Grade: A)

Instructor: Self-directed learning with self-selected literature pairings. Collaborated with owner of Ozzie's Organic Farm and 4-H leader Olivia Harriet.

Mode/Frequency: Hands-on activities alone and in groups, varying in length from 2–15 hours weekly.

Description:
- Learned organic farming methods
- Gained knowledge of natural pest-control techniques
- Explored soil ecology and its importance
- Read books on soil science and its impact on the environment
- Explored the concept of farming as an ecosystem
- Learned about river pollution and its connection to farming methods
- Observed the impact of farming on local waterways
- Gained practical experience in planting and maintaining an organic garden
- Learned Prezi presentation software

Course materials: Field participation at Ozzie's Organic Farm, the Ohio River, and backyard garden. Read *The Soil Will Save Us* by Ohlson, *The Farm as Ecosystem* by Brunetti, and *Soil* by Evans.

Evaluation criteria: 25% hands-on work, 50% reading and discussion, 25% final 15-minute, multimedia presentation to 4-H group on implementing sustainable farming practices.

Activity 6.1: Sample Course Description Template

Refer to the records you developed in Chapter 4. In this activity, you will distill those records to their pithy core in a concise summary. Use the following template to create your description.

Course Title (school year*, credit, grade in class*)
Instructor: Mode/Frequency: Description: Course materials/resources: Evaluation criteria:

*Year and grade may be useful but are optional as they are already included on the transcript.

Summary

Regardless of how traditional or eclectic your student's learning has been, a targeted course description helps admission readers better understand the tone and flavor of your homeschool. Parents can usually upload the course description document along with the transcript when completing the counselor side of college applications. Some universities require this sort of elaboration while others strongly encourage it. Even if course descriptions are not required by a college, skipping them can result in unanswered questions about your curricular choices. Excellent course descriptions enhance applications.

CHAPTER 7

Homeschool Profile

Contextualize Your Homeschooling Decisions

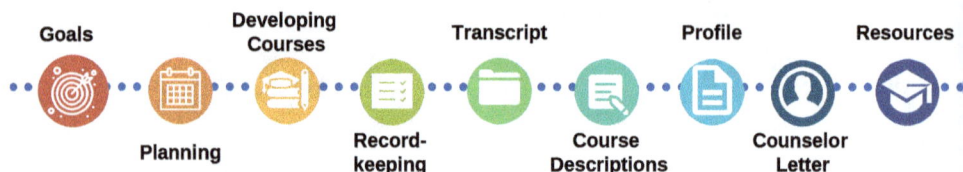

Goals • Developing Courses • Transcript • Profile • Resources

Planning • Record-keeping • Course Descriptions • Counselor Letter

In this chapter, you will learn how a descriptive school profile helps admission readers understand the particulars of your homeschool. You will answer key questions to clarify your philosophy, your approach, and your student's academic readiness.

According to the National Association for College Admission Counseling (NACAC), nearly three-quarters of schools include a school profile to contextualize their students' transcripts. Admission officers read transcripts from a large number of schools. The school profile provides a framework for understanding what was available to students. Admission professionals rely on this supplemental information when considering individual applicants.

A homeschool profile should be clear and easy to digest at a glance. Keep the document to no more than two focused pages. Rather than writing long paragraphs, consider whether boxed sections might better direct attention. Bullet points can highlight important information. A well-placed graphic or photo may be effective. NACAC provides links to many institutional school profiles if you are interested in browsing options for your layout.

NACAC provides more 1,200 links to school profiles.
https://www.nacacnet.org/school-profiles/

When done well, a homeschool profile strengthens an application by providing readers with a fully-fleshed accounting of why you and your student chose to homeschool.

To create your homeschool profile, you will work through four steps:

1. **Include essential demographics:** You will learn what information an admissions office likely already knows and what you need to explain.
2. **Describe your philosophy:** You will describe your "why" for homeschooling.
3. **Explain grading scales and graduation requirements:** You will help admission readers understand your student's grades, graduation qualifications, and college readiness.
4. **Introduce educational partners and providers:** You will contextualize any outside entities you included as part of your homeschooling.

Throughout this chapter, we will examine a case study of one homeschool family and their school profile as well as several sample descriptions of educational providers. At the end of the chapter, review the entire example homeschool profile the way an admission officer might. What did you learn about the homeschool program and student? What more would you like to know? How would this school profile influence your decision to admit or not admit the student?

Step 1: Include Essential Demographics

Admission offices often employ data analytic systems and enrollment yield consultants to help them market to students. As a result, colleges and universities know much about applicants simply from their zip codes. Admission offices likely know what sorts of opportunities are available and expected in your area.

However, colleges and universities likely will not know what resources are available to *homeschoolers* in your town. Feel free to use the demographic section to inform readers of how popular homeschooling is in your municipality, note any significant homeschool community opportunities or lack thereof, and give a sense of how diverse the homeschooling population might be (see Figure 7.1). Provide informative details, such as major industries in your region or the research climate in your town, if these elements are relevant to your student's experiences.

Figure 7.1: Example of Homeschool Profile Demographics Section

Bay View Academy is located in Norfolk, Virginia, within the Norfolk City Public Schools District boundaries. Lake Taylor High School serves as the local public school.

The homeschooling community in the Hampton Roads area draws from a diverse population with regard to socioeconomic status, ethnic background, religious faith, and educational goals. Many families have members that serve the military. Homeschooling in Hampton Roads, an online cyber-support group, has over 11,000 online members and promotes clubs, classes, and co-ops in the area. We opted for secular opportunities within our co-op choices.

Activity 7.1: Defining Your Homeschool Community

Now it's your turn. Jot down the key characteristics you want readers to know about homeschooling in your community.

My Local Area	Notable Homeschool Characteristics
Popularity of homeschooling	
Types of homeschooling groups	
Local homeschool special-interest clubs	
Limitations/challenges of local homeschool opportunities	

Step 2: Describe Your Philosophy

Homeschooling is no longer a novel choice. Indeed, on October 31, 2023, *The Washington Post* estimated that the number of homeschoolers in the United States was between 1.9 and 2.7 million for the 2022–23 academic year. Admission offices have been evaluating homeschoolers for decades and possess a broad understanding of some reasons people homeschool. That said, share your family's homeschooling philosophy with admissions officers rather than relying on their assumptions. Use what you wrote in Chapter 1 of this book as the basis for your philosophy.

Often, both "pull" reasons (the benefits of homeschooling) and "push" reasons (poor fit or problems at an institutional school) contribute to a parent's decision to homeschool. Some families—especially families of color, LGBTQIA+ families, and allies—might want to protect their children from harmful systemic elements. Many home educators want to present a different or more diverse view of academic subjects than what is presented by a standard textbook. Maybe a student's educational requirements cannot be met in the public or private setting and so a parent turns to homeschooling to meet a specific need for acceleration or remediation. Some families want their students to experience an unhurried childhood full of rich exploration with room to puzzle, wonder, and learn. Some teens opt to homeschool to make time for the development of a special talent and practice in acting, the arts, music, or sports. All of these are entirely valid reasons to list in your philosophy section.

Figure 7.2: The Pull Factors of Homeschooling

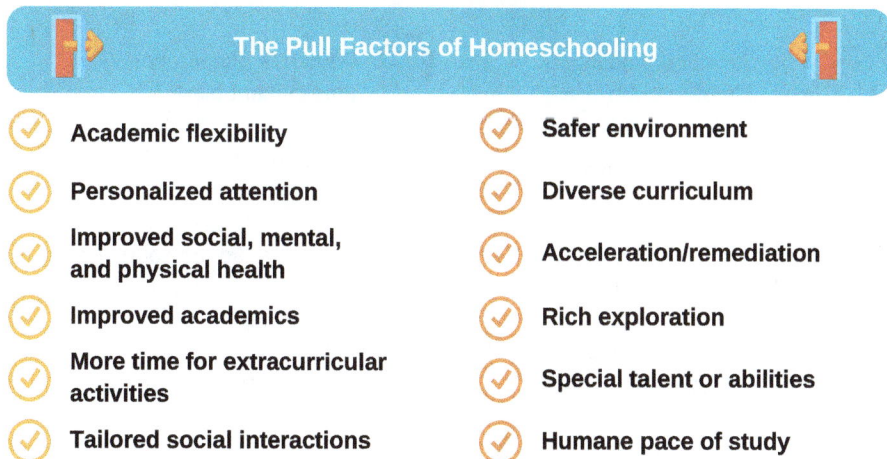

The Pull Factors of Homeschooling

- ✓ Academic flexibility
- ✓ Personalized attention
- ✓ Improved social, mental, and physical health
- ✓ Improved academics
- ✓ More time for extracurricular activities
- ✓ Tailored social interactions
- ✓ Safer environment
- ✓ Diverse curriculum
- ✓ Acceleration/remediation
- ✓ Rich exploration
- ✓ Special talent or abilities
- ✓ Humane pace of study

Whatever your reasons might be, let colleges know. Be mindful of tone. It is possible to state a "push" reason matter-of-factly without sounding critical of school systems. Emphasize your "pull" reasons so readers will focus on the benefits your child experienced through homeschooling.

Also address how your choices supported your objectives. If you value critical thinking, for example, that may explain why social studies courses included a detailed research paper each year. For many families, balancing individual, self-initiated learning with group class opportunities remains a priority. You might note that balance in your philosophy section.

In addition to discussing academics, your philosophy section can explain the development of your teen as a whole person in the context of your family's values. You might prioritize internships or apprenticeships, volunteer service, a part-time job, or a rich slate of extra-curricular activities. Share the choices that contribute to your philosophy.

In light of test-optional policies, including a statement about your stance on testing and the availability of test seats makes sense. Not all admission officers understand that Advanced Placement (AP) exam seats can be difficult for many homeschoolers to obtain, especially for those who qualify for accommodations.

Activity 7.2: Philosophical Questions to Answer

Work through the following questions to help you refine and hone the philosophy you developed in Chapter 1:

? What is your animating principle/overall aim?

? What role did part-time employment play?

? What is your curricular focus?

? What role did volunteer service play?

? What varieties of educational activities did you use?

? What role did mentoring/internships/apprenticeships play?

? What role does the pursuit of extracurricular activities play?

Look carefully at Figure 7.3 to see how our example home educator addressed these questions in her philosophy section of the homeschool profile.

Figure 7.3: Example of Homeschool Philosophy Section

Bay View Academy spans grades 4 through 12. Prior to fourth grade, each student attended a Children's House Montessori classroom. These Montessori roots influenced the educational philosophy of Bay View Academy in that:

- Children are natural learners.
- Achievement follows educational opportunities that encourage spontaneous cooperative inquiry.
- Freedom in education develops self-confidence and independence.
- This approach fosters inner discipline that respects self and cares for others.

Allowing Evan the opportunity to develop his passion for learning and operate at his own pace informed our educational philosophy.

We followed a classical model, integrating subjects and coordinating among them, with academics at home and enrichment at a local co-op. Math was taught individually to fit Evan's instructional level and learning style. Language arts emphasized classical literature and included activities that were rich and engaging. History focused on using primary source documents for a deeper understanding. Science and art used a hands-on, discovery approach.

Extracurricular activities supported interests and enhanced skills in fencing, tennis, swimming, soccer, music theory, and orchestra. Joining a multi-age co-op allowed Evan to participate in creative projects, additional science labs, public speaking opportunities, and group presentations. These multi-age groupings also encouraged learning and leading to take place naturally and cooperatively.

Step 3: Explain Grading Scales and Graduation Requirements

Grades and rigor remain top considerations for most college admissions offices. Your homeschool profile should clearly explain your grading scale and those of outside providers so admission readers will interpret them accurately. NACAC's 2020 "Best Practices for Developing a School Profile" recommends careful explanation because "absent detailed information about a school's grading system, colleges may be prone to draw conclusions on their own."

Help colleges understand your grading scale in its proper context. If your outside providers used different grading scales, detail each one. Figure 5.5 will help you convert letter or number grades. If you graded your student's written work for some courses but not for others, use the profile to explain the different grading systems. Your homeschool profile will also explain the overall grading philosophy you developed in Chapter 4. We provide an example in Figure 7.4.

Figure 7.4: Example of Grade Description Section

Grading and Academic Success
We incorporated external evaluations including AP exams and dual enrollment classes into all major categories of academics: English Language Arts, math, sciences with labs, social sciences, and languages other than English. When possible, we incorporated College Board–approved courses or university or community college coursework. Grades were based on a variety of evaluation methods and included narration, participation, project work, and testing. We used a 100-point grading scale.

Your transcript should include a note about weighting (see Chapter 5: Transcripts), and the grading section of the profile offers the chance to delve into more details about weighting. For example, you might designate a class as honors level and give the grade corresponding weight. This section of the homeschool profile is where you can explain your criteria. In institutional schools, honors courses tend toward a higher degree of mastery and greater independence on the part of the student. In home education, if a class meets three or more of the criteria in Figure 7.5, you can probably safely give it honors weighting and credit.

Figure 7.5: Honors Criteria Chart

Core subject area	Required significant self-discipline and/or time	Used above grade-level resources
Took the AP exam and earned 3 or higher	Demonstrated a high level of independence and initiative	Produced work of quality far above a typical high school course requirement

Note: Educators must undergo an AP Course Audit to officially label a class as AP. If a class covers AP material but did not undergo the audit, you may give it honors designation.

After explaining your grading scale, mention your basic graduation requirements as well as whether and how your homeschooler exceeded the minimum (see also Chapter 2: Planning Your Homeschool Requirements).

Step 4: Introduce Educational Partners and Providers

The educational partners and providers section offers a higher-level view than your course descriptions do. Course descriptions provide details about each class while the educational partners section of a homeschool profile introduces each outside provider.

Don't assume admission readers will be familiar with the co-ops, online providers, or community offerings in your area. Known entities such as community colleges and four-year colleges and universities used for dual enrollment require less explanation than do homeschool-focused outside providers. Still, consider drawing attention to any special recognition that the outside provider school received or its unique mission (see Figure 7.6).

Figure 7.6: Sample Dual Enrollment Provider Description

North Central College is a four-year liberal arts and science college located in Naperville, IL. The college is one of five in the world recognized with a 2015 Senator Paul Simon Award for Comprehensive Internationalization. Its 3,000 students study in more than 65 undergraduate and graduate programs.

Kai Nez is a Community Scholar (via a dual enrollment program) and took the classes How to Read and Write Poems (ENGL 106), Investigating Biology (BIOL 106-1), and Introduction to Environmental Science (BIOL 195-2) in person at North Central College.

Homeschool providers often offer their own descriptions of their organizations, so you may not need to create your own blurb. Consider where your energy might be best spent. For instance, picking and choosing snippets from the homepage of one popular AP provider could yield this description:

Pennsylvania Homeschoolers AP Online (AP Homeschoolers Inc.) has 25 years of experience providing interactive online AP classes, with more than 1000 students enrolled in classes during the last school year. Almost 3/4 of students earn top grades of 4 (25%) or 5 (48%) on the AP exams that they take.

Other providers might provide a description when asked. Jaime Smith, who runs Online G3, offers this description of that program:

OnlineG3 offers online classes with live weekly webinars for gifted and twice-exceptional learners. History and science classes focus on critical thinking, student inquiry, and primary source analysis. Language arts classes are de-stranded so that literary analysis is done separately from grammar and writing to allow for asynchronous development of skills. Online G3 is regionally accredited by the Western Association of Schools and Colleges (WASC).

As you can see, provider descriptions should be tightly focused, between two and four sentences in length. Any longer risks diluting the narrative. Think of a partner description as a meaty soundbite.

Some families may have an extensive number of outside partners, and including all of them would make the profile unwieldy. If that is your case, consider providing an overview of the types of providers in your homeschool profile instead. You might note that mentors, online providers, co-ops, community colleges, clubs, and teams all contributed to your child's education. You could then include specific mention of a few entities within your course descriptions.

Activity 7.3: Educational Partners Descriptions

List and describe any outside providers you used.

Type of Providers	Name(s) of Provider(s)
College (dual enrollment)	
High school	
Online Course Provider	
Homeschool Co-op or Group	
Club/Team	
Other	

Figure 7.7 offers a completed homeschool profile. This parent used two standard-size pages to cover the elements described this chapter in a concise way.

Figure 7.7: Example of a Complete Homeschool Profile

Bay View Academy Homeschool Profile

Our Community

Bay View Academy is located in Norfolk, Virginia, within the Norfolk City Public Schools District boundaries. Lake Taylor High School serves as the local public school.

The homeschooling community in the Hampton Roads area draws from a diverse population with regard to socioeconomic status, ethnic background, religious faith, and educational goals. Many families have members that serve the military. Homeschooling in Hampton Roads, an online cyber-support group, has over 11,000 online members and promotes clubs, classes, and co-ops in the area. We opted for secular opportunities within our co-op choices.

Our Philosophy

Bay View Academy spans grades 4 through 12. Prior to fourth grade, each student attended a Children's House Montessori classroom. These Montessori roots influenced the educational philosophy of Bay View Academy, in that:

- Children are natural learners.
- Achievement follows educational opportunities that encourage spontaneous cooperative inquiry.
- Freedom in education develops self-confidence and independence.
- This approach fosters inner discipline that respects self and cares for others.

Allowing Evan the opportunity to develop his passion for learning and operate at his own pace informed our educational philosophy.

We followed a classical model, integrating subjects and coordinating among them, with academics at home and enrichment at a local co-op. Math was taught individually to fit Evan's instructional level and learning style. Language arts emphasized classical literature and included activities that were rich and engaging. History focused on using primary source documents for a deeper understanding. Science and art used a hands-on, discovery approach.

Extracurricular activities supported interests and enhanced skills in fencing, tennis, swimming, soccer, music theory, and orchestra. Joining a multi-age co-op allowed Evan to participate in creative projects, additional science labs, public speaking opportunities, and group presentations. These multi-age groupings also encouraged learning and leading to take place naturally and cooperatively.

Educational Partners

Norfolk Academic Guild is a homeschool collective that strives for excellence through academic rigor. Live classes meet weekly and are taught by subject area specialists. The highest level of classes offered through Norfolk Academic Guild is Honors and AP. Evan took five of the five Honors classes, and five of the five AP classes available. Educational opportunities spilled over into the experiential through group field trips to aquariums, zoos, museums, and local theater events. Evan participated in Norfolk Academic Guild all four years of high school.

Online Providers

We chose the following providers for their academic rigor.

- **Harvard Medical School HMX Online** courses focus on bringing medical science concepts to life via real-world and clinical applications. Evan's curiosity motivated him to apply for both the Biochemistry and Pharmacology courses. While appropriate for medical students and medical professionals, Evan successfully managed both courses and expects to receive a Certificate of Achievement for each.

- **Clover Valley Chemistry** offers full-year (36 week), online high school chemistry courses for homeschooled students. These courses are taught by an experienced high school and college chemistry instructor with over 20 years of teaching, tutoring, and homeschooling experience. Evan's Organic Chemistry course was recommended for students who might be considering a career in medicine or another professional field.
- **The Lukeion Project** offers live online, high-quality, college preparatory Classical subjects taught by experienced credentialed educators. Evan achieved a Gold Medal on the National Latin Exam for both Latin I and Latin II.
- **Derek Owens** offers math and physics courses for homeschool students with online and live classes. Evan took Geometry, Algebra II and Trigonometry, and Pre-Calculus all at the Honors level.

In-person Dual Enrollment

- **Virginia Wesleyan University** offered Evan the opportunity to take Calculus I and II, Human Anatomy and Physiology, and several German classes, including three 300-level courses.
- **Tidewater Community College (TCC)** allowed Evan to enroll in Chemistry 111 and Chemistry 112 prior to high school. These classes are designed for science and engineering majors. Evan achieved a grade of A in both classes. Evan continued with additional classes at TCC including Economics and History classes.

Grading & Academic Success

We incorporated external evaluations including AP Exams and dual enrollment classes into all major categories of academics: English language arts, math, sciences with labs, social sciences, and languages other than English. When possible, we incorporated College Board–approved courses or university or community college coursework. Grades were based on a variety of evaluation methods and included narration, participation, project work, and testing. We used a 100-point grading scale.

Summary

Now that you have thought through the different sections of the homeschool profile, you can compile your document. Review your draft profile because your homeschool may have unique elements not covered here. The homeschool profile presents an opportunity for you to provide nuance for admission readers who want to understand the opportunities and challenges of homeschooling in your setting. What might raise questions for an admissions reader? Make sure you answer those queries in your homeschool profile or your counselor recommendation.

CHAPTER 8

Counselor Recommendation

Endorse Your Student Enthusiastically

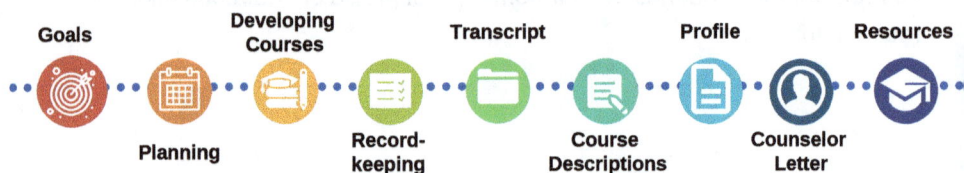

Goals   Developing Courses   Transcript   Profile   Resources

Planning   Record-keeping   Course Descriptions   Counselor Letter

The counselor recommendation feels like the capstone project for a homeschooling parent. The transcript, course descriptions, and homeschool profile state the facts of what a student accomplished, and the counselor's letter provides context for why the student accomplished those things, how they exhibited growth, and who they are as a college-ready learner. This recommendation also operates as a FAQ document, addressing questions that might arise when admissions officers read the application.

As you reflect on your child's educational journey and look at them as a young adult, you may shed some tears. Allow for the emotions involved in writing this final document. This is a time of transition for both you and your student. Be gentle with yourself as you work through this final piece of documentation.

When you begin, consider your student's strengths. Jot down a list of the characteristics you want to convey and tuck it away to allow yourself time to process. When you create your first draft, you may be tempted to dwell on the beginning of your educational journey. Although a childhood anecdote might set the stage, remember that colleges are focused on your student's high school years as those years best predict who your student will be in college. Your letter should fill in any gaps from the student side of the application and offer nuance that your student may not be able to recognize or verbalize.

Homeschoolers often wonder how seriously colleges consider a counselor recommendation written by a family member. No one can give an overarching sense of a student's educational path like the home educator who guided and facilitated all aspects of their child's education. Although teacher recommendations should come from others, it is entirely appropriate and expected for the home-educating parent to write the counselor letter. Admission readers understand that the homeschool counselor recommendation is not coming from an entirely neutral observer, and they still use this letter to inform and broaden their understanding of the student.

You will follow four steps to write and submit your counselor recommendation:
1. **Channel emotion effectively:** You will inventory your recent anecdotes and quotes.
2. **Identify distinctive qualities:** You will highlight your student's strengths and growth.
3. **Create maximum impact:** You will design a visually appealing recommendation that covers any information missing from other parts of the application.
4. **Conquer the Common Application:** You will learn to navigate the counselor side of the Common App.

Step 1: Channel Emotion Effectively
In all likelihood, you possess a storehouse of stories about your student. Now is the time to take inventory of those anecdotes. Look for examples that show strengths through action and detail. What lasting image of your student do you want colleges to form?

If you are having difficulty choosing among multiple strengths and stories, consider having your student complete a values inventory like the free VIA Survey. For each of your child's top four to five strengths, jot down a specific instance of how they recently demonstrated that strength. Highlight moments that do not show up in other places on the application. Figure 8.1 lists some sample character traits. Activity 8.1 will help you identify examples of your student demonstrating key traits.

VIA Character Strengths Survey
https://www.viacharacter.org/

Figure 8.1: Sample Character Traits

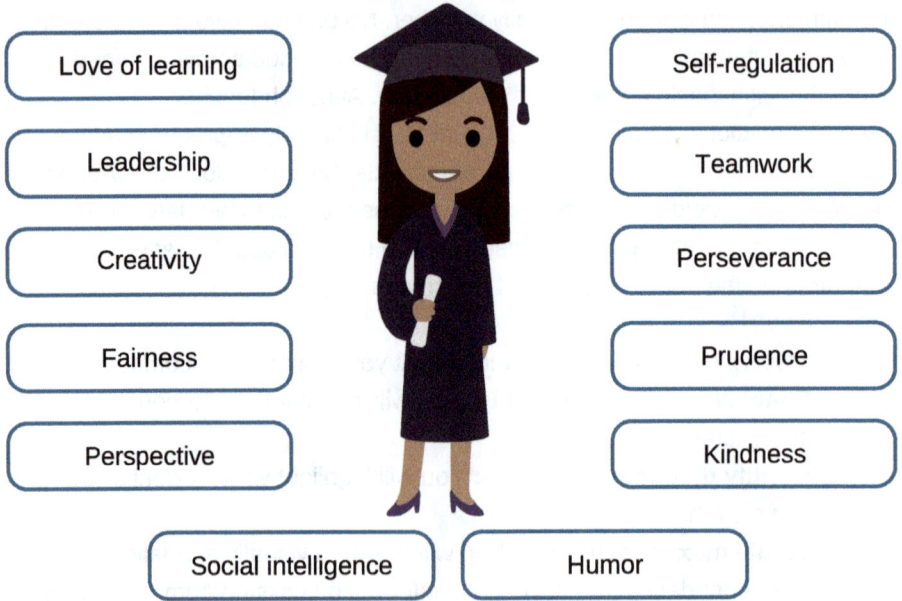

Love of learning	Self-regulation
Leadership	Teamwork
Creativity	Perseverance
Fairness	Prudence
Perspective	Kindness
Social intelligence	Humor

Activity 8.1: Demonstrating Your Student's Character Traits

Complete the following chart by writing down four or five of your student's strengths. Beside each one list an example of a way your teen demonstrated that strength during the high school years.

Strength	Example

The counselor recommendation promotes your student's readiness for college. This is not a place to list moments of adult-teen conflict or to dwell on poignant childhood moments. Although a description of how a student addressed an area of weakness can be helpful to admission readers, the counselor letter should primarily point to the unique positive qualities of the student.

Feel free to weave the words of others into your letter. Have you kept a brag file on your teen? You might share some insightful comments from outside teachers, coaches, neighbors, employers, or mentors. Review emails, congratulatory speeches, or text messages that provide additional insights on your student. Record them in the following chart.

Activity 8.2: Short Quotes from Others About Your Student

Person and Role	Quote with Date Received

Review the collected quotes to scan for relevance. Do any of them attest to the academic and personal characteristics of your child in a way that is not demonstrated elsewhere in the application? Consider which could be most useful in your recommendation. If an example from earlier years conveys something important, look for a recent example that demonstrates the same quality.

Step 2: Identify Distinctive Qualities

In "Tips for Writing Student Recommendations," the College Board encourages counselors to "start with an image that the body of your recommendation develops." Some categories to address include:

- Your student's approach to learning: What motivates them? How is this evident in your homeschooling and how will it translate to college?
- Your child's progression of ownership and agency in learning and living: What specific examples support what you're saying?
- Your student's personal growth: What specific ways did your child show initiative and impact?
- Your teen's strengths: What academic, leadership, or character strengths did your student exhibit?
- Your student's resilience: How did they address specific challenges they faced during high school?

Do not recreate your teen's transcript or activities list in this section. Instead, provide context.

Figure 8.2: Categories to Address

Approach to learning	Educational progression	Personal growth	Strengths	Overcoming challenges

Note: University admissions officers shared these tips about counselor recommendation letters:

"We need to be directed to the things that are most important for us to understand about a student. More importantly, these should be things the student didn't tell us, or at least given from a perspective the student does not have about themselves." —Georgia Tech

> "The goal here is to give the admission committee context for the student's achievements. For example, 'John has taken AP Biology, AP Physics and AP Chemistry' should be 'John is one of only two students in our local homeschool group who has taken AP Biology, AP Physics, and AP Chemistry.' This small measurable statement changes the story for John; context is everything!" —The University of Dallas

The counselor recommendation can be a place to explain any extenuating circumstances affecting a student throughout high school. If a family member faced serious illness or if an extended period of unemployment limited the resources available for homeschooling, those are worth mentioning. If a student experienced circumstances that hindered their ability to perform academically, a matter-of-fact statement about the situation and how it was resolved helps admission readers make sense of the transcript and school profile. If your child faced a challenge and worked to overcome it, you may want to highlight that as a strength—especially if the skills gained will serve them well in college.

Step 3: Create Maximum Impact

Admission readers have limited time and must move through applications with efficiency. To make it easier for them, consider breaking up solid blocks of text into smaller paragraphs. Georgia Tech Admission Blog advises, "Many of you are considering using bullet points in your letters...it's really helpful for us to hone in on the information you want to highlight." Text boxes, highlights, and italics also draw readers' eyes to key points.

Aim for a one-page counselor letter; do not exceed two pages. Your first drafts may be considerably longer. Ask one or two trusted people who know your child well to provide feedback. Some admission office systems now use AI to summarize recommendations. Consider running your letter through one of the available AI options and asking it to summarize the contents. Does the summary match what you're trying to convey? Trim anything less relevant so you can focus on the most important characteristics. Be concise and specific and use strong verbs and nouns. Section headers, bullet points mixed with narrative elements, and boldfaced key phrases all help create an engaging document that leaves no doubt about key takeaways.

Figure 8.3: Effective Elements of a Counselor Letter

| Easy-to-read format | Well-edited | Key information highlighted | Concise length |

Figure 8.4 shows the counselor recommendation for a particular student. Shawntay wanted to study marine biology in college. Her parent highlighted Shawntay's strong interest in the natural world, compassion, creativity, and ability to meet challenging situations. Each story provided details and context, while honestly addressing Shawntay's emerging skills and the family stressors that affected her homeschooling. When you're done reading through this letter, use Activity 8.4 to create your own counselor recommendation.

Figure 8.4: Counselor Letter of Recommendation Example

Homeschool Academy   **Recommendation for Shawntay**

<u>Distinctive Qualities</u>

Passion and compassion are hallmarks of Shawntay's character. She is committed to social justice and is a **fierce defender of others' rights**. She is protective of her younger siblings and proactive in ensuring her disabled friend's needs are met and the friend's food restrictions respected.

Shawntay recently held back six lanes of traffic so that a mother duck and ten baby ducklings could safely cross to a pond. She is **unfailingly kind** to every living creature that she encounters. She **sees situations through the eyes of others** - human and animal - and shares that viewpoint through **powerful writing**. One writing coach commented that Shawntay's way of "explaining animal behaviors from the animals' perspective can be eye-opening for a person who hadn't considered those motivations before."

We tailor Shawntay's home education to her wide-ranging passions. A **voracious reader**, Shawntay devours everything from dystopian fiction to biographies to texts on psychology and ecology. She **makes connections between seemingly unrelated topics**. For example, she enjoys digitally designing historically accurate costumes from different periods inspired by wild bird species' colors and body shapes. She spent over 100 hours last fall researching and making her own historically accurate Halloween costume.

Shawntay sets **challenging goals** and works to achieve them; she completed **SCUBA certification** at the age of 13 and found **paid employment** at a fast food restaurant during the pandemic, for example.

Challenges and Areas of Development

Social situations can be difficult for Shawntay, yet she participates in and leads group activities such as a cyber security tournament and a pioneering competition. Participation in Scouts helped her overcome a fear of public speaking through repeated practice. She even gave an off-the-cuff speech at a recruitment event.

Also, Shawntay has a sibling with significant special needs and behavioral challenges; this requires additional levels of forbearance and maturity from Shawntay.

Academic and Intellectual Growth

- A **leading member of the Homeschool Science Olympiad** team throughout middle and high school years, Shawntay takes on additional events for the benefit of the team. Shawntay won **regional medals** in 6 events and **advanced to the state competition**.
- Computer Graphics teacher Ms. Booth comments, "Shawntay goes out of her way to give her classmates positive feedback and **goes well above and beyond all expectations**."
- Professor Massey of Local College described Shawntay's writing as "**very ambitious and engaging**."
- Last year, Shawntay's graphic art piece "Title" in the **NPTSA Reflections Art Competition** advanced first to **State and then to National level**.
- English teacher Ms. Engel commented: "Your **unique perspective** broadened my thinking…a truly **thought-provoking analysis**."

Activities, Interests, and Areas of Impact

- Shawntay earned the rank of **Eagle Scout** in under 2 years, part of the **Inaugural Class of Female Eagle Scouts**.
- She completed a **12-day, 110-mile backpacking trek**.
- Shawntay was awarded a **Fearless Girl Scholarship** to attend National Youth Leadership training, part of the first cohort of females.
- Shawntay is a devoted **foster caregiver** to kittens born to feral mothers, preparing them for a future as adoptable pet cats. The adoption agency turns to her for shy or nervous "spicy" kittens.

Additional Comments:

Shawntay is an exceptional candidate for college, strong both in character and in academics. She approaches everything with integrity and verve.

Activity 8.3: Create Your Counselor Recommendation

Now it's your turn. Use the following template to write a first draft of your counselor letter for your student.

Last Name Homeschool
Counselor Recommendation for Student Name

Distinctive Qualities
[One to two paragraphs with specific strengths backed by particular examples.]

Academic and Intellectual Growth
[Quotations from outside teachers in specific courses can be a nice touch. Specific detail is key.]
- [Add bullet points here]

Activities, Interests, and Areas of Impact
[List tangible areas of impact that demonstrate growth and progressive responsibility. Are there any areas not covered in other places on the application? Highlight them here. Use specific, concrete details.]
- [Add bullet points here]

> **Additional Comments**
> [Are there any extenuating circumstances that should be detailed? Are there any important details that don't fit in another category? Feel free to highlight these in a brief paragraph.]
>
> Sincerely,
> [Your Name Here]
> [Contact Information]

The counselor recommendation is usually the last of the four core documents that home educators write. When you finish the polished version of this recommendation, we hope you celebrate! This is a huge accomplishment. A student marks a milestone when they complete their K–12 journey, and homeschooling parents achieve their own milestone when their child graduates.

Step 4: Conquer the Common Application

Now that you've completed your core documentation, you need to submit it to the colleges your student is applying to. In this section, we discuss the most frequently used application: the Common Application. For colleges that use their own application platforms, you will find similar requirements.

The Common App was created to simplify the college application process by giving students one application that can be sent to multiple colleges. More than 1,000 colleges and universities accept this application.

Your student initiates the Common App by creating their student account. After your student attaches a school to their Common App account and waives their FERPA rights, they can invite you to be their counselor. You will then get an email from the Common App that tells you how to make a counselor account.

> The Common App is used by more than 1,000 colleges and universities around the world. The Common Application also provides students with a variety of resources.
> www.commonapp.org

Home educators may not create a counselor account prior to receiving this invitation from the student.

The counselor side of the Common App contains some questions that do not typically apply to homeschoolers. You may skip the questions that are not required and are not designed for a homeschool setting.

Currently, three required homeschool counselor questions allow for responses up to 1,000 words:

- Please provide any information about the applicant's homeschool experience and environment that you believe would be helpful to the reader (e.g. educational philosophy, motivation for homeschooling, instruction setting, etc.).
- Please explain the grading scale or other methods of evaluation.
- If the student has taken courses from a distance learning program, traditional secondary school, or college, please list.

Since you will have already covered those topics in your School Profile and Course Descriptions, you can give brief answers here and direct readers to the appropriate documents for full details.

The Common App gives instructions about where to upload your School Profile and Counselor Recommendation. It does not specify how to share your course descriptions; you should use the Transcript section to upload both the transcript and the course descriptions. You can create a single PDF that contains the one-page transcript followed by the pages of course descriptions or upload them as two separate documents.

Once you submit your documents you can no longer change them, and they become available to all colleges your student applies to through the Common App. If you discover any substantive errors after submission or if your student's senior year plans change, do not despair. You can use the optional report feature once to send corrections or to provide any updates or changes. A mid-year report is required by some colleges; they will notify students and provide a due date. For the mid-year report, provide an updated transcript with fall-term grades. At the end of the year, submit your student's final transcript to the college or university that your student chooses to attend. There is typically no need to submit a diploma to colleges or universities, but you can create and sign one to present to your student to commemorate their graduation. Preserve copies of the final documents in a safe storage space.

Summary

As you completed the units in this workbook, you defined your goals for what a personalized homeschool experience might look like for your incredible teen's high school years. You balanced meeting requirements with addressing areas of interest and incorporating learning from a wide variety of sources. Tracking grades required you to think deeply about what mastery looked like in the context of your homeschool. Finally, you documented your student's learning by creating a transcript, course descriptions, homeschool profile, and a counselor recommendation to help colleges understand your student's educational path.

Congratulations! You did it!

SOURCES & RESOURCES

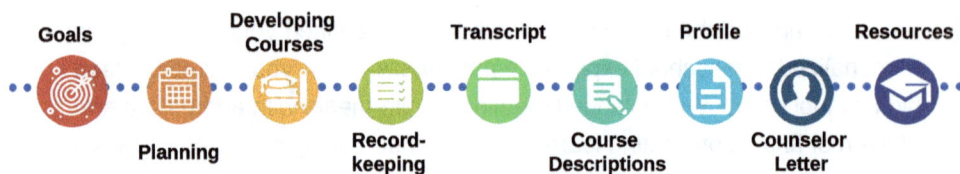

Goals · Developing Courses · Planning · Transcript · Record-keeping · Course Descriptions · Profile · Counselor Letter · Resources

All website links were accessed and active as of May 24, 2024. Note that websites and links may change. For each chapter, sources cited are listed first, followed by relevant resources.

Introduction
- *The Washington Post*. "Home schooling's rise from fringe to fastest-growing form of education." October 31, 2023.
  https://www.washingtonpost.com/education/interactive/2023/homeschooling-growth-data-by-district/
- National Center for Education Statistics. "Fast Facts: Homeschooling."
  https://nces.ed.gov/fastfacts/display.asp?id=91
- Aurora Institute. "Moving from Seat-Time to Competency-Based Credits in State Policy."
  https://aurora-institute.org/blog/moving-from-seat-time-to-competency-based-credits-in-state-policy-ensuring-all-students-develop-mastery/
- Johns Hopkins Institute for Education Policy. "Homeschool Hub."
  https://education.jhu.edu/edpolicy/policy-research-initiatives/homeschool-hub/

Chapter 1
- Julie Bogart. *The Brave Learner: Finding Magic in Homeschool, Learning, and Life*, page 1.
  https://store.bravewriter.com/products/the-brave-learner
- University of Nebraska-Lincoln. "Thoughtful Learning: What are the 4 C's of learning skills."
  https://newsroom.unl.edu/announce/csmce/5344/29195
- Shanterra McBride and Rosalind Wiseman. *Courageous Discomfort*.
  https://www.courageousdiscomfort.com/

- Structural Learning. "Multisensory Learning In The Classroom: A Teacher's Guide."
  https://www.structural-learning.com/post/multisensory-learning-in-the-classroom-a-teachers-guide
- Paula Penn-Nabrit. *Morning by Morning: How We Home-Schooled our African-American Sons to the Ivy League.*
  https://paulapenn-nabrit.com/books/morning-by-morning/
- Akilah S. Richards. *Raising Free People: Unschooling as Liberation and Healing Work.*
  https://raisingfreepeople.com/

Chapter 2

- New York State Education Department. "Home Instruction."
  https://www.nysed.gov/nonpublic-schools/home-instruction-questions-and-answers
- Washington State Legislature. "Home Education."
  https://app.leg.wa.gov/RCW/default.aspx?cite=28A.225.010
- Washington State Board of Education. "Graduation Pathway Options."
  https://www.sbe.wa.gov/our-work/graduation-pathway-options
- ProPublica. "Homeschooling Regulations By State."
  https://projects.propublica.org/graphics/homeschool
- Florida State University. "What We're Looking For."
  https://admissions.fsu.edu/first-year/WWLF/
- Education Commission of the States. "50-State Comparison: High School Graduation Requirements 2023; All Data Points."
  https://reports.ecs.org/comparisons/high-school-graduation-requirements-2023
- Tennessee Department of Education. "English Language Arts Standards."
  https://www.tn.gov/education/districts/academic-standards/english-language-arts-standards.html
- Colorado College. "The Block Plan."
  https://www.coloradocollege.edu/basics/blockplan/
- National Collegiate Athletic Association. "Core Courses."
  https://www.ncaa.org/sports/2014/10/6/core-courses.aspx

Chapter 3

- Forbes. Profile of Dashiell Young-Saver.
  https://www.forbes.com/profile/dashiell-young-saver/?sh=6ac5c5bb2c34
- Dr. Gholnecsar "Gholdy" Muhammad. *Cultivating Genius: An Equity Framework for Culturally and Historically Responsive Literacy*, page 145.
  https://shop.scholastic.com/teachers-ecommerce/teacher/books/cultivating-genius-an-equity-framework-9781338594898.html

- Heritage Homeschoolers Book Club.
  https://heritagemom.com/heritage-homeschoolers-book-club/
- Amber O'Neal Johnston. *A Place to Belong: Celebrating Diversity and Kinship in the Home and Beyond,* pages 57, 27.
  https://heritagemom.com/belong/
- Commonwealth of Massachusetts Division of Fisheries and Wildlife. "Apply to become a licensed wildlife rehabilitator."
  https://www.mass.gov/how-to/apply-to-become-a-licensed-wildlife-rehabilitator
- New York State Department of Environmental Conservation. "Wildlife Rehabilitator License."
  https://www.dec.ny.gov/permits/25027.html
- Center for Professional Education of Teachers. "Unpacking Curriculum: Adopt, Adapt, Apply."
  https://cpet.tc.columbia.edu/news-press/unpacking-curriculum-adopt-adapt-apply

Chapter 4

- NCAA Eligibility Center. "Home School Toolkit."
  http://fs.ncaa.org/Docs/eligibility_center/Student_Resources/Home_School_Toolkit.pdf
- Cornell University Center for Teaching Innovation. "Using Rubrics."
  https://teaching.cornell.edu/teaching-resources/assessment-evaluation/using-rubrics
- AP Central. "Course & Exam Pages."
  https://apcentral.collegeboard.org/courses
- Rubistar. "Create New Rubric."
  http://rubistar.4teachers.org/index.php?screen=NewRubric&module=Rubistar
- American Association of Colleges and Universities. "VALUE Rubrics."
  https://www.aacu.org/initiatives/value-initiative/value-rubrics

Chapter 5

- University of Massachusetts Amherst. "First Year Admission Requirements."
  https://www.umass.edu/admissions/undergraduate-admissions/apply/first-year-students/first-year-admissions-requirements
- Robert Kunzman and Milton Gaither. "Homeschooling: An Updated Comprehensive Survey of the Research."
  https://icher.org/
- The College Board. "SAT Scores and Privacy."
  https://satsuite.collegeboard.org/sat/scores/k12-educators/score-reports/scores-privacy

SOURCES & RESOURCES

- BigFuture. "How to Convert (Calculate) Your GPA to a 4.0 Scale." https://bigfuture.collegeboard.org/plan-for-college/get-started/how-to-convert-gpa-4.0-scale
- GPA Calculator. "High School GPA Calculator." https://gpacalculator.net/high-school-gpa-calculator/
- Khan Academy. "Sample school report and transcript (for homeschoolers)." https://www.khanacademy.org/college-careers-more/college-admissions/applying-to-college/applying-as-a-homeschooler/a/sample-homeschool-transcript
- NCAA Eligibility Center. "Home School Transcript Information." http://fs.ncaa.org/Docs/eligibility_center/Student_Resources/Home_School_Transcript_Example.pdf

Chapter 6
- Eric Hoover. "Working Smarter, Not Harder, in Admissions." March 12, 2017. https://www.chronicle.com/article/working-smarter-not-harder-in-admissions/
- Learning Corner. "Subject Explorer: Discover Your Student's Learning." https://learningcorner.co/subject-explorer
- Bryn Mawr College. "Homeschooling and Alternative Education Students." https://www.brynmawr.edu/admissions-aid/admissions-aid-policies/homeschooling-alternative-education-students

Chapter 7
- National Association for College Admission Counseling. "School Profiles." https://www.nacacnet.org/school-profiles
- *The Washington Post.* "Home schooling's rise from fringe to fastest-growing form of education." October 31, 2023. https://www.washingtonpost.com/education/interactive/2023/homeschooling-growth-data-by-district/
- Age of Learning. "The Homeschooling Movement Explained." https://www.homeschoolplus.com/learn/research/exploring-homeschooling-movement
- National Association for College Admission Counseling. "Best Practices for Developing a School Profile." April 2020. https://www.nacacnet.org/best-practices-for-developing-a-school-profile/
- Vanderbilt University. "Application Process: First-year." https://admissions.vanderbilt.edu/apply/first-year-process/

Chapter 8

- VIA Institute on Character. "VIA Character Strengths."
  https://www.viacharacter.org/
- The College Board. "Tips for Writing Student Recommendations: Counselors."
  https://counselors.collegeboard.org/college-application/writing-recommendations-counselors
- Georgia Tech Admission Blog. "Freshman Application Review – The Nuts and Bolts (part 2 of 2)."
  https://sites.gatech.edu/admission-blog/2017/10/12/freshman-application-review-the-nuts-and-bolts-part-2-of-2/
- University of Dallas. "Admission Requirements: Non-Accredited & Self-Designed Homeschool Student."
  https://udallas.edu/admissions-aid/undergraduate/admission-requirements.php
- The Common Application.
  https://www.commonapp.org/